Socially Responsible Innovation in Security

This book examines the possibility of socially responsible innovation in security, using an interdisciplinary approach.

Responsible innovation in security refers to a comprehensive approach that aims to integrate knowledge related to stakeholders operating at both the demand and the supply side of security – technologists, citizens, policymakers and ethicists. Security innovations can only be successful in the long term if all the social, ethical and ecological impacts, and threats and opportunities, both short term and long term, are assessed and prioritized alongside technical and commercial impacts.

The first part of this volume focuses on security technology innovation and its perception and acceptance by the public, while the second part delves deeper into the processes of decision-making and democratic control, raising questions about the ethical implications of security ruling.

This book will be of much interest to students of critical security studies, sociology, technology studies and IR in general.

J. Peter Burgess is Professor and Chair of Geopolitics of Risk at the École Normale Supérieure, France, and Adjunct Professor at the Centre for Advanced Security Theory (CAST) at the University of Copenhagen, Denmark.

Genserik Reniers is a Full Professor at the Engineering Management Department of the University of Antwerp in Belgium, and at the Safety and Security Science Section of the Delft University of Technology in the Netherlands.

Koen Ponnet is an Assistant Professor at IMEC-MICT, Ghent University, Belgium.

Wim Hardyns is an Assistant Professor at the Institute of International Research on Criminal Policy (IRCP) in the Department of Criminology, Criminal Law and Social Law, Ghent University, Belgium.

Wim Smit is a former army chaplain at the Belgian army, and the Director-General of Wereld Missie Hulp, a Flemish development organization.

Series: Routledge New Security Studies
Series Editor: J. Peter Burgess
École Normale Superieur (ENS), Paris

The aim of this book series is to gather state-of-the-art theoretical reflection and empirical research into a core set of volumes that respond vigorously and dynamically to new challenges to security studies scholarship. This is a continuation of the PRIO New Security Studies series.

Security Expertise
Practice, power, responsibility
Edited by Trine Villumsen Berling and Christian Bueger

Transformations of Security Studies
Dialogues, diversity and discipline
Edited by Gabi Schlag, Julian Junk and Christopher Daase

The Securitisation of Climate Change
Actors, processes and consequences
Thomas Diez, Franziskus von Lucke and Zehra Wellmann

Surveillance, Privacy and Security
Citizens' perspectives
Edited by Michael Friedewald, J. Peter Burgess, Johann Čas, Rocco Bellanova and Walter Peissl

Socially Responsible Innovation in Security
Critical Reflections
Edited by J. Peter Burgess, Genserik Reniers, Koen Ponnet, Wim Hardyns and Wim Smit

Visual Security Studies
Sights and Spectacles of Insecurity and War
Edited by Juha A. Vuori and Rune Saugmann Andersen

For more information about this series, please visit: www.routledge.com/Routledge-New-Security-Studies/book-series/RNSS

Socially Responsible Innovation in Security
Critical Reflections

Edited by J. Peter Burgess,
Genserik Reniers, Koen Ponnet,
Wim Hardyns and Wim Smit

LONDON AND NEW YORK

First published 2018
by Routledge
2 Park Square, Milton Park, Abingdon, Oxon OX14 4RN

and by Routledge
711 Third Avenue, New York, NY 10017

Routledge is an imprint of the Taylor & Francis Group, an informa business

© 2018 selection and editorial matter, J. Peter Burgess, Genserik Reniers, Koen Ponnet, Wim Hardyns and Wim Smit; individual chapters, the contributors

The right of the editors to be identified as the authors of the editorial matter, and of the authors for their individual chapters, has been asserted in accordance with sections 77 and 78 of the Copyright, Designs and Patents Act 1988.

All rights reserved. No part of this book may be reprinted or reproduced or utilized in any form or by any electronic, mechanical, or other means, now known or hereafter invented, including photocopying and recording, or in any information storage or retrieval system, without permission in writing from the publishers.

Trademark notice: Product or corporate names may be trademarks or registered trademarks, and are used only for identification and explanation without intent to infringe.

British Library Cataloguing-in-Publication Data
A catalogue record for this book is available from the British Library

Library of Congress Cataloging-in-Publication Data
A catalog record for this book has been requested

ISBN: 978-0-8153-7139-7 (hbk)
ISBN: 978-1-351-24690-3 (ebk)

Typeset in Times New Roman
by Wearset Ltd, Boldon, Tyne and Wear

Contents

List of figures	vii
List of tables	viii
Notes on contributors	ix
Acknowledgements	xii

Introduction: responsible innovation in security – setting the scene 1

J. PETER BURGESS, GENSERIK RENIERS, KOEN PONNET,
WIM HARDYNS AND WIM SMIT

1 Danger, innovation, responsibility: imagining future security 12

J. PETER BURGESS

PART I
Security technology, public perception and acceptance 23

2 Drones – dull, dirty or dangerous? The social construction of privacy and security technologies 25

MARC VAN LIESHOUT AND MICHAEL FRIEDEWALD

3 The influence of technological innovations on theft prevention: perspectives of citizens and experts 44

KIM VAN HOORDE, EVELIEN DE PAUW, HANS VERMEERSCH
AND WIM HARDYNS

4 When it rains in Paris, it drizzles in Brussels? 63

HANS VERMEERSCH, ELLEN VANDENBOGAERDE AND
EVELIEN DE PAUW

vi *Contents*

PART II
Public and private decision-making 83

5 **Securitization by regulation? The Flemish mayor as**
democratic anchor of local security policies 85
TOM BAUWENS

6 **Raising the flag: the state effects of public and private**
security providers at East Jerusalem's national parks 97
LIOR VOLINZ

PART III
Democratic control and ethical implications 115

7 **Evaluation and effectiveness of counter-terrorism** 117
FIONA DE LONDRAS

8 **The bleak rituals of progress; or, if somebody offers you a**
socially responsible innovation in security, just say no 129
MARK NEOCLEOUS

Index 141

Figures

2.1	Number of projects from FP5, FP6 and FP7 with 'privacy' and/or 'security' mentioned in their objectives	30
2.2	Relative keyword usage over time	31
2.3	Relative keyword usage over time	31
6.1	Private armed escort at the entrance to the City of David National Park	102
6.2	Guardhouse above a Jewish-Israeli settlement compound in Silwan	106
6.3	The Old City's Dung Gate	109

Tables

2.1	Factors driving and hindering technology development and use	32
4.1	Sample profile	71
4.2	Changes in attitudes between 2014 and 2016	71
4.3	Average differences between 2014 and 2016, P values for differences (one-way ANOVA), effect of wave, controlling for demographic differences and respective P values	72
4.4	Average differences between respondents that had a terror or control frame in 2016 and effect of this frame, controlling for demographic differences	73
4.5	Average differences according to time of completion, and effect of arrest of Salah Abdeslam, controlling for demographic differences	74
5.1	Overview of the interpretative repertoires	90

Contributors

Tom Bauwens is a postdoctoral researcher at the research group Crime & Society (CRiS) in the Department of Criminology, Vrije Universiteit Brussel. His research and teaching interests centre around the policy and politics of prevention, crime control and local security practices.

J. Peter Burgess is a philosopher and political scientist. He is Professor and Chair of Geopolitics of Risk at the École Normale Supérieure, Paris, and Adjunct Professor at the Centre for Advanced Security Theory (CAST) at the University of Copenhagen. He is Series Editor of the Routledge New Security Studies collection. His research and writing concern the meeting place between culture and politics, especially in Europe, focusing in particular on the theory and ethics of security and insecurity.

Fiona de Londras is the inaugural Chair of Global Legal Studies at the University of Birmingham, a post she took up in 2015 following three years as Professor of Law at Durham University. She writes widely on counter-terrorism, constitutionalism and human rights, and has (co)authored or (co)edited 10 books and yearbooks and approximately 60 articles and book chapters on these themes.

Evelien De Pauw works as an assistant and PhD candidate since 2016 at Ghent University, Faculty of Economics and Business Administration, Department of Public Administration, Research Group of Governing and Policing Security (GaPS). She is also a guest lecturer at VIVES University College. Her main research topics are technology and innovation processes, security networks and the governance of security.

Michael Friedewald, EngD is a senior research fellow at the Fraunhofer Institute for Systems and Innovation Research ISI in Karlsruhe Germany and leads the ICT research group. His recent work focuses on the privacy and data protection challenges of future and emerging information and communication technologies. He is also working in the field of foresight and technology assessment. He has coordinated several FP7 projects including PRESCIENT, SAPIENT and PRISMS. He is co-editor of *Privacy and Security in the Digital Age* (Routledge, 2014) and *Surveillance, Privacy and Security: Citizens' Perspectives* (Routledge, 2017).

x *Contributors*

Wim Hardyns is an Assistant Professor at the Institute of International Research on Criminal Policy (IRCP) in the Department of Criminology, Criminal Law and Social Law, Ghent University, Belgium. His current interests are crime mapping and statistics, environmental criminology, crime prevention, new security technologies, big data, radicalization and terrorism.

Mark Neocleous is Professor of the Critique of Political Economy at Brunel University, UK. He is the author of a number of books, most recently *War Power, Police Power* (2014) and *The Universal Adversary: Security, Capital, and 'The Enemies of All Mankind'* (2016). He is currently working on a book on *The Politics of Immunity* and a co-authored work on the manhunt.

Koen Ponnet is Assistant Professor and Researcher at IMEC-MICT of the Faculty of Political and Social Sciences of Ghent University. His main research interests are the (mental) health, risk and problem behaviour of adolescents and adults, both offline and online.

Genserik Reniers obtained a Master of Science degree in Chemical Engineering at the Vrije Universiteit Brussel and received his PhD in Applied Economic Sciences from the University of Antwerp. He founded the Antwerp Research Group on Safety and Security (ARGoSS) in 2006 and was appointed part-time full professor at the University of Antwerp, responsible for safety and risk teaching and research. In October 2013, he was appointed in a part-time capacity as a full professor at the Safety Science Group of Delft University of Technology in The Netherlands.

Wim Smit, PhD in Moral Theology, obtained his doctorate at KU Leuven with a dissertation on the topic of 'violations of civil and human rights in the fight against terrorism'. He wrote several (opinion) articles and books on the theme and has a blog (https://veiligheidenrechten.wordpress.com). In 2005 he edited an English book on *Just War and Terrorism*, and in 2007 he published his first book in Dutch: *Rechtvaardige oorlog en terrorisme: Recht en onrecht in tijden van terreur*. In February 2015 another book was published: *Onveilige burger bange politiek? Van 9/11 tot Snowden en verder*. For more than 13 years he was a chaplain in the Belgian army, but since the beginning of 2015 he has been Director-General of Wereld Missie Hulp.

Marc van Lieshout, MSc, is Senior Scientist at the Nederlandse Organisatie voor Toegepast Natuurwetenschappelijk Onderzoek (TNO). He works within the TNO Department of Strategy & Policy on privacy and identity management issues, looking especially at strategic and policy perspectives. He is Business Director of the Privacy and Identity Lab, a knowledge centre of TNO, with Dutch universities Tilburg and Nijmegen. He acted as Programme Manager of TNO's programme on the societal impact of ICT from 2005–2012, and is now managing the knowledge part on privacy and e-identity. He was a visiting scientist at JRC-IPTS from July 2008–July 2009. He has been engaged in several (inter)national projects on the assessment and evaluation of national and international activities related to privacy and data protection, for the European Commission, the European Parliament and national departments. He has been actively engaged with the FP7-project PRISMS. His research interests are on innovation policy and privacy, including regulatory, business and societal processes.

Ellen Vandenbogaerde joined the Research Centre for Social Innovation at Vives University College, after graduating from the University of Sussex with a PhD in Development Studies. Before that she obtained an MA in Criminology from Ghent University and worked as a social and political researcher for various companies in England. Her interests centre around security studies, urban sociology, youth violence, inequality, governance and research methods.

Kim Van Hoorde conducted the project 'The Influence of Technological Innovations on Theft Prevention – A Citizen Perspective', and started as a researcher at the Vives University College at the beginning of October 2014 after her Master Studies in Criminology and Advanced Master's in Conflict and Development. This one-year project was recommended by the Directorate Local Integral Security of the Federal Government Service Internal Affairs and accomplished in cooperation with the University of Antwerp. Promoters of the project are Evelien De Pauw (Vives), Hans Vermeersch (Vives) and Wim Hardyns (University of Antwerp).

Hans Vermeersch works as a senior researcher at the Vives University College, Centre of Expertise in Social Innovation, Research Group Society & Security, Doorniksesteenweg 145, 8500 Kortrijk, Belgium, hans.vermeersch@vives.be.

Lior Volinz is a PhD candidate at the Amsterdam Institute for Social Science Research (AISSR) at the University of Amsterdam. His research focuses on the privatization and pluralization of security and military functions in Jerusalem and their relation to the (re)production of differentiated citizenship in a divided city. Lior can be contacted at l.volinz@uva.nl.

Acknowledgements

This collection of essays emerged out of a two-day workshop held at the University of Antwerp in October 2015. This interdisciplinary workshop aimed at moving beyond the techno-centric and security focus to investigate the social, ethical and organizational impacts of the security business, to understand the implications for individuals and the nature of society and to gain insight into how security norms are embedded in cultural norms. The two-day workshop brought together over 20 researchers from Europe to discuss their research projects.

We are grateful to all who presented papers in the original workshop and to everyone who attended. We owe gratitude to the whole team at the University Centre Saint-Ignatius Antwerp for organizing the workshop and for making this volume possible. Special thanks are due to our authors for taking part in the project and making this volume possible.

Antwerp, September 2017

Introduction

Responsible innovation in security – setting the scene

J. Peter Burgess, Genserik Reniers, Koen Ponnet, Wim Hardyns and Wim Smit

Few question today the notion that innovation is a core thrust of modernity. Innovation – the sustained introduction of the new – is more than a principle, more than a norm, more than a value. It is a primary assumption of our time, a milestone indicating the inevitable rise in the quality of life in society – sometimes paradoxically measured in quantitative terms, the guarantee that life should and will continuously improve, that the present is better than the past and that the future will be better than the present. The expectation is so imposing that one might even say that the new is old, that it has always been so and thus that that innovation is paradoxically obsolete. Innovation is such a powerfully present supposition that it has become indiscernible and thereby de-politicized and de-socialized.

Responsible innovation in security refers to the comprehensive approach of guiding security innovation in a manner such that all stakeholders, involved in the process of such innovation in some way, can obtain knowledge at an early stage on the consequences of the outcomes of their decisions and actions and on the range of options open to them, letting them effectively evaluate both outcomes and options in terms of societal needs and moral and ethical values.

As an example, in security innovation, an important ethical value in society that promptly comes to mind is the concern of many citizens about privacy. It has traditionally not been straightforward for engineers and technicians to include privacy as an essential factor in the design phase of novel security technologies. Technicians are mainly concerned with technological innovation and managers with economic success. Nonetheless, societal stakeholders concerned with responsible innovation obviously require security innovators to take moral issues such as privacy into consideration in the design phase, as well as other ethical factors such as fairness, equity, safety, ergonomics, environmental impacts and the like (Grinbaum and Groves, 2013).

The purpose of this book is to integrate knowledge about responsible innovation related to stakeholders operating on the demand side of security: technologists, citizens, policy makers and ethicists. It develops the hypothesis that the failure of innovative solutions and approaches to meet with societal and citizens' needs can only be avoided by true responsible innovation. A number of well-known innovative technologies that have been contested on ethical grounds are,

2   *J. Peter Burgess* et al.

for instance, nanotechnology, genetically modified organisms, nuclear technology and military innovations. If such innovations are not responsible, and do not take ethical aspects into account in the earliest stages, investment can be weakened or lost as a consequence of lack of a 'license to exploit the innovation' by society, and hence by policy makers. Moreover, innovations with respect to security (related to e.g. theft, terrorism, military operations, etc.) will likely always be in the interest of citizens and thus be under the attention of public stakeholders, if only because of their intrinsically public nature. Security innovations can only be successful in the long term if their social, ethical and ecological impacts, and threats and opportunities, both short term and long term, are assessed and prioritized alongside technical and commercial impacts, and if the security innovators are transparent about the approach and decisions.

The discussion on responsible innovation engages a broad and growing field of scholarship. Research carried out in this field sets itself apart by its unique proximity to private industry and to the new partnerships between industry and public organizations, known under the blanket concept of the 'public–private partnerships'. Considerable public resources are at present being mobilized and redirected towards initiatives carried out under this banner. While a range of benefits for innovation are often rehearsed by supporters of public private partnerships – including flexible financing arrangements, tailored legal arrangements, hybrid labour practices and tailored tax incentives – the most significant impact of combing resources into such partnerships is the redistribution of risk.

It is a commonplace of innovation science that financial risk does not map directly onto innovation risk. Obviously, large-scale innovation requires large-scale financial support; however, the risks taken in innovation tend to belong to a different order of danger and a different kind of uncertainty. De Saille and Medvecky (2016), for example, translate the notion of responsibility into purely economic terms, judging its success and failure in terms of the growth or stagnation it provokes. Large-scale, sustainable innovation requires more than finance alone; it also carries a distinct moral thrust. By interpreting the notion 'responsibility' as a moral term with strong normative valence, as do, for example, Pelle and Reber (2015), innovation becomes a far more subjectively oriented matter, a philosophical enterprise with deep cultural roots and directions. Here even 'corporate socially responsibility' is less inclined towards the societal means and ends of innovation than with the social ethics that it powers.

Responsible innovation is an activity deployed through the wide range of consultative practices it is obliged to attend to. In practice it is a novel form of cultivating the points of contact between society and the technologically oriented industries that interface with it; namely, the interplay between the social structures, political institutions, shared commercial activities and common fields of social interaction like schools, religious institutions and local cultural traditions. Commercial innovation must be new, reaching beyond the status quo, while at the same time maintaining a link to its imbedding. Even in the cases where it does not explicitly seek to advance or put into play the cultural values and social norms of the society in which it is operating, it must engage with them. For this

Introduction 3

reason concern for the efficiency of innovation processes warrants a direct approach. Indeed, some argue that the communities involved directly in innovation processes must solicit the perspectives and opinions of society and bring together the many audiences, and their knowledge in the activity of scientific and technological decision-making (Van Oudheusden, 2014, pp. 70–73).

Responsible innovation is in this sense a bridging and integration mechanism. Its success lies not only in its ability to generate technologically viable solutions but to manage the tensions between involved stakeholders. Similarly, outcomes are not measured merely by their ability to bring novel technological solutions that plug into a societal configuration or a cultural or political setting; rather, they have to function and provide results – in the case of security this implies integrating with the particular insecurities of society. Innovation must innovate by engaging with the conservative forces in society around long-standing and sometimes ensconced expectations. Technological success does not automatically imply innovation (Bozeman, 2007; Bozeman and Sarewitz, 2011).

The new discourse of responsible innovation is marked deeply by its imposing intransitivity: Grammatically, 'innovation' has no object. It is a verbal action without an object of action. It is an action unto itself, a relation of subjectivity, of the subject to the self. Innovation does not externalize; it expands the internal, deploying the self, the logic, the discourse, the materials of the self, into the world. It is never purely fresh, purely new; it is always re-combinatory, a jumbling or shuffling of the civilizational code of what is already or has already been but perished. In a strict sense one can reasonably ask whether innovation in any refined form is thinkable when its raw materials are necessarily the materials of the past. Innovation is a system only partially opened to the new, to what is new, to what can change. Innovation is a system of endogenous possibilities and endogenous dangers. This is true not only for the actual material foundations on which innovation must stand – the existing technologies, the actual natural and human resources, and most prominent, the values that determine and predetermine the moral and political frames of reference and the horizon of possibilities for thinking new values. If, as many argue today, a primary aim of all innovation is the creation of value, then this value system must be seen in continuity with those that come before it and those from which it cannot be separated.

The matter of value is of course the core of innovation. Time passes; the past flows ceaselessly towards the future. There is change. And yet when can one say that this change has taken the form of innovation? If there is an experience of time, if time has passed, then it is only because there is a difference between the present and the past, between now and before. To ascertain this there must be a qualitative measure of difference, of the experience of change. This change is calibrated as a change of value. Successful innovation corresponds to the creation of value, itself measured in a number of ways. The correlation of success metrics is irregular and on occasion disruptive, pitting value systems against each other, and highlighting clashing assumptions of what science itself is, what its role is in society, where and how it is accountable and 'responsible'. Market success, the easiest and inevitably first-order metric of innovation, guarantees

4   *J. Peter Burgess* et al.

neither technological results nor fruitful public benefit from the research and development involved in innovating; that is, the furtherance or preservation of widely accepted public values such as safety, privacy and choice. As Valdivia and Guston suggest, innovation is fraught with paradoxes and trade-offs: innovation has simultaneously advanced and undermined public values dear to democratic societies (2015, p. 6).

Progress is not continuous, but rather fragmented, moving in fits and spells, buffeted by the flows of finance, political economy, technology, fashion and culture. These forces amplify and dampen the variations in interpretation and in the application of public values in decision-making on public policy. This is a source of the 'third tension shaping the governance of innovation', the one which opposes experts to citizens, and corresponds to differences in ways that public values are internalized and then concretized in the different spheres (2015, p. 7).

Responsible innovation can and must also be regarded from another perspective, from another angle. Not only can the political and ethical argument be made that innovation, which is in and of itself neither responsible nor irresponsible, should indeed be responsible. But responsibility itself can quite naturally be regarded as an object of innovation. 'Responsibility' can also be regarded not as an autonomous regulatory checklist but as the object of a critical gaze, subject to review and revision, to innovation and improvement. A critical angle on responsible innovation can also question the character of the responsibility in responsible innovation. As Stilgoe, Owen and Macnaghten have clarified, responsibility towards science implies a responsibility towards society as well. To the degree that responsible innovation focuses on developing responsible technological approaches to challenges and possibilities, they must also foresee evolving risks in the social sphere. Innovative societal governance is, however, of a fundamentally different order than the governance of technologies. The 'dilemma of control' generated by the very notion of societal innovation redoubles complexity and with it, responsibility (2013). Not least, quickly developing technologies create 'institutional voids' by simple virtue of the fact that they engage a new form of responsibility. Governance implies responsibility, even when it is invoked implicitly or tacitly. Thus, according to Stilgoe, Owen and Macnaghten, innovation implies an additional innovation of anticipating the societal impact of yet unseen and still unforeseeable products of innovation (2013, pp. 1574–1577).

Innovation is thus widely conceived as a situation within a set of extant public values. This implies a recognition of these values and acceptance that some component of public values constitutes a starting point with the innovative ethos. Public values are never entirely innovated: they are a signpost, an index for a path that has a continuity starting well before the moment of innovation and ostensibly ending well after it. It is thus, in terms of Taebi *et al.*, a recognition of a set of values, but not entirely an endorsement of it. Engaging with public values is regarded as a way of preserving them in order to make partial use of them, or even negate them while at the same time preserving them (Taebi *et al.*, 2014, pp. 118–120).

From this mid-level interaction with public values, we may also move to the macro-view and a layer of questions about responsibility to society at large. As

Stahl has pointed out, responsible innovation is not only a question of the implication and impact of those directly present in an immediate or concrete innovation; it can also be raised as a question of the orientation of society as such – its 'grand challenges' such as employment, well-being, growth, societal coherence, development and democracy (Stahl, 2013, p. 2). In this sense the responsibility of responsible innovation can refer to the core well-being of members of society, to the reinforcing or re-casting of the core principles and practices of society and of democracy itself. It can be applied as a tactical approach to counteracting the negative effects of the 'fragmentation of moral authority' due to other evolving tendencies that are perceived as threats to society (Appleyard and Stahl, 1995; Davies, Glerup and Horst, 2014). It can also provide a regulatory measure for the governance of private sector actors, to their vulnerabilities to the changing relationship between the market and society (Sholten and van der Duin, 2015). This perspective on responsible innovation links it with the logic of economic growth and the complex link between technological development and the economics of inflation and stagnation (De Saille and Medvecky, 2016, pp. 7–10).

Certain segments of the discourse of responsible innovation reformulate the challenges as linked to personal values of individuals in society. Pelle and Reber, for example, take pains to show the relationship between intersubjective value positions and the technological changes that structure society as a whole. They regard responsible innovation as a question of personal responsibility and moral agency. Corporate-level responsibility is in this sense linked to individual responsibility. The concept of responsibility, according to this perspective, can be clarified through the methods of moral philosophy, 'which defines responsibility as role, task, capacity, authority, virtue, responsiveness, obligation, accountability, blameworthiness, liability', since the moral sphere of responsibility 'begins before and goes beyond legal frontiers, ethical concerns frequently arise before new laws have been discussed or enacted' (2015, p. 113).

These processes become socially – but also politically, culturally, morally – more complex when it is security that lies at the heart of the innovation. As several contributors point out, the call for security – securitization – is among the most powerful forces for innovation that we know. It has left a significant mark on the way that innovation is considered, justified and put into practice. Surveillance of society is of course not simply one security measure among many, but rather among the most powerful and consequential of them all. Surveillance innovation is consequentially more contentious than most, often even regarded as being at odds with democratic principles (De Jong, Kupper and Broerse, 2016, p. 27).

As becomes clear through the contributions to this volume, for example in chapters by Burgess and van Lieshout and Friedewald, the European Commission regards responsible innovation as key support for an overall agenda of free trade, growth and industrial innovation that aligns with the principles of the European liberal project, which is couched in principles of fairness and rights. Through the channel of the European liberal project, the concept of responsible innovation has found its way into European Commission research and development and the Framework research programmes.

6 *J. Peter Burgess* et al.

> The Science Shop model of participatory research and innovation has been successful in bringing students, researchers and civil society together towards tackling real issues at the local and regional levels. Aside from positively impacting on the co-creation of solutions to real world problems, the process of engaging with society has strengthened both the research process and its outcomes, thereby contributing to research excellence and acceptability of innovation outcomes.
>
> (European Commission, 2016, p. 11)

From a theoretical point of view it is simple to map the liberal progress-oriented, technological-valorized, econometrically governed virtues of responsible innovation onto the principles of European Construction, from the Schuman Declaration to the Maastricht Treaty. The European Union is the prototype of responsible innovation, itself a model for all other responsible innovations. It addresses gender imbalances, inequalities, principles for freedom, equality and dignity. It both symbolizes and nurtures science. It is for these reasons that the European Commission was a front runner in both funding and organizing research under the banner of 'responsible innovation'. According to the 2013 European Commission plan, the notion of responsible innovation is not only a virtue associated with innovation in general, emphasizing 'responsible' approaches to it, but it is also implicit in the logic of invention, novelty and transformation. It links to the general challenge of integrating ethics into research to address social needs and meet the 'grand challenges' of our time. It assumes that innovation will be contested, thus calling on the ability to make value-based decisions beyond mere questions of feasibility (European Commission, 2013). Among the challenges which the Commission associates with responsible innovation is that associated with the speed of technological change. Because of bureaucratic and procedural slowness, conventional regulation cannot adapt quickly enough to remain relevant. The time-lag effect is exacerbated by the more intense difficulties in predicting technological advances, giving rise to what von Schomberg has identified as the 'Collingridge dilemma'; that is, ethical issues that would ordinarily be addressed early on in the design process are not foreseen and thus not addressed in time to make a meaningful difference (2011, p. 8). Responsiveness is thus regarded as the key element, and innovation itself, which von Schomberg defines as 'a transparent, interactive process by which societal actors and innovators become mutually responsive to each other with a view on the (ethical) acceptability, sustainability and societal desirability of the innovation process and its marketable products' (2011, p. 11; also Gardner and Williams, 2015). In this sense, according to Owen, Macnaghten and Stilgoe (2012, pp. 3–4) or Blok and Lemmens (2015, pp. 23–24), responsible innovation means first and foremost creating the space of possibility for this kind of dialogue and exchange. The more rarefied concerns of social ethics, the good life and the rights of the individual follow from this basic principle. Moreover, the forum thus created will make possible the necessary predictive adaptability to societal ethical concerns.

Introduction 7

Today, public debate is centred on emerging technologies such as mentioned above (nanotechnology etc.); however, discussion about innovative security solutions is rapidly gaining interest due to the recent iconic terrorist attacks; that is, the 9/11 terrorist attacks in New York in 2001, the Madrid and London attacks of 2004 and 2005 respectively, and the most recent attacks in Paris (2015) and in Brussels (2016). Security technologies of interest are, for instance, innovative cameras, all kinds of identification technology or body scanners, drone technology, smart sensors for security purposes, etc. It is essential that a shared understanding of the appropriate behaviour of the authorities, governments, businesses, NGOs and researchers is developed and achieved for such technologies. A joint understanding and perspective on responsible security innovations is indeed basic for gaining and maintaining the trust and confidence of the public and stakeholders.

Responsibility should not be seen as a barrier to security innovation, but, on the contrary, as an incentive for its success. Sustainable development and use of security innovations require an involvement of society in the creation of its vision, the articulation of its values and use, and the making of the innovation itself. Nonetheless, one should realize that sometimes difficult and unpopular decisions have to be taken. Involving stakeholders and the public at large at an early stage, thus upstream, does not guarantee that there will not be differences of opinion between them. However, responsible innovation ensures clear and effective communication about the decisions taken and about the influences having led to the chosen options. As such, the decision-making process concerning security innovations is legitimate, inclusive and transparent, which will undoubtedly build confidence in the process, even if stakeholders don't always agree with the consequences.

These themes, their discourses and discordances, are developed in the chapters of this book, structured according to three main lines of current reflection on security and innovation: (1) security understood as technological innovation, and the tension between the public sphere and its own perception and acceptance of security technologies; (2) the public and private decision-making processes that support and legitimate security innovation; and (3) the democratic and ethical suppositions and implications of the innovation as an ideal of governance.

The volume is opened by J. Peter Burgess, who situates the question of responsible innovation in its broader cultural context. That context is one in which security and technological innovation, liberalism and an intensified values discourse converge to legitimize new forms of policing and social control. These new societal forms, Burgess notes, in turn solicit new technologically based protections through new and innovative technical security solutions. The chapter reveals 'responsible innovation' as both a concept and a political strategy, with an ambivalent, even contradictory relationship with the process of modernization. The chapter inquires into what responsible innovation has gained or lost in relation to the modern project of innovation, and suggests that while granting itself a new lease of life through the notion of responsibility, innovation – particularly in its European reincarnation – pays the price of discarding the moral, cultural or even spiritual dimensions that make innovation responsible. It concludes by asking whether the very concept of innovation is itself under innovation relative to its predecessors.

8 *J. Peter Burgess* et al.

The technological dimensions of this dilemma are further concretized in Part I, 'Security technology, public perception and acceptance', which is opened by Marc van Lieshout and Michael Friedewald. While privacy and security are often considered to be traded off against each other, these authors propose a perspective on privacy and security that regards them as two sides of the same coin. They present material from a four-year EU research project that studied the way that privacy and security are designed into systems meant to secure airports, to assist the police in detecting hooligans in a football stadium or aggressive protestors during a demonstration, or to check for signs of radicalism on social media. Based on an institutional analysis over a period of ten years of security and privacy research in the European Research Area, they showed the dominance of security over privacy in institutional settings, roadmaps and research activities concerning security and privacy. The analysis is complemented by a sociotechnical analysis of the ways privacy and security considerations are addressed by designers during the product development process. The authors examine the ongoing discourse of privacy and security in the design process and show how privacy and security are inscribed in early stages of the design process as well as into the discourse of space used by designers and in the technical systems that result from the design process.

The next chapter, 'The influence of technological innovations on theft prevention: perspectives of citizens and experts', looks at how technological innovations designed to improve theft prevention are received by citizens and experts. Kim Van Hoorde, Evelien De Pauw, Hans Vermeersch and Wim Hardyns argue that while the internet and innovative technologies are opening up tremendous possibilities for governments and their citizens, they also facilitate the carrying out of crimes. In their chapter they present results from a study including measures involving home automation, biometrics and track-and-trace. They survey the impact of such systems on citizen expectations and acceptance and on the overall sustainability of security technologies. Their results indicate that while individuals have their own perceptions and visions, preventative security measures adapt to their pre-existing attitudes rather than to objective and correct information. This permits the authors to conclude that technological features should not be regarded as a black box tool to achieve security. Instead, they are the requirement of securing technological systems in themselves. As a consequence, citizens are called to understand the basic concepts, possibilities and limitations when applying the internet and new technologies, as for now they are easy targets by means of their open and unprotected virtual – and hence physical – doors.

The following chapter, 'When it rains in Paris, it drizzles in Brussels?' by Hans Vermeersch, Ellen Vandenbogaerde and Evelien De Pauw, evaluates the impact of terror attacks on perceptions concerning the use of surveillance-orientated security technologies (SOSTs) by the Belgian government. The chapter assesses the common assumption that citizens are more inclined to support government measures that risk limiting their privacy when they are invoked in the wake of terror attacks. The study focusses on public perceptions among Belgian students following the events of 2015 in Paris and beyond, based on a survey comparing the attitudes towards the use of SOSTs in 2014 and in 2016, after a year in which terror attacks dominated the headlines. The analysis indicates that respondents are indeed more inclined to accept potentially privacy-intruding government measures, and that risk perception (though not fear of crime and trust in public authorities) increased, with exceptions, between 2014 and 2016. Nonetheless, the analysis suggests that this result does not necessarily translate into increased acceptance of SOSTs. A more detailed view suggests that public opinion on the use of SOSTs defies a simple privacy–security trade-off.

Part II of this volume, 'Public and private decision-making', opens with Tom Bauwens' study of local security policy, 'Securitization by regulation? The Flemish mayor as democratic anchor of local security policies'. The chapter examines in detail the modern social imaginary, and in particular the view that prevails that security is the raison d'être of liberal democratic governments, which we tend to hold responsible for ensuring public order and security in the name of the common good. As a consequence it becomes clear that security is arguably the most potent and dangerous of all policy goals. Public order and security are considered legitimate goals to restrict fundamental rights, albeit temporarily. Yet, according to the European Convention of Human Rights, these restrictions are only legitimate when they are in accordance with the law and necessary in a democratic society. Crucially, however, the use of the 'security label' does not necessarily reflect whether a problem is a security problem – in the sense of a real, 'objective' existential threat. Bauwens' chapter analyses the restraining orders issued by mayors to ban individual 'troublemakers' from attending certain parties, nightclubs and pubs in the municipality. These restraining orders emerged at the local level but have recently been institutionalized and explicitly included in the federal municipal law. The chapter concludes that regulating the pursuit of security does not suffice, but rather that law is only one of the repertoires used by mayors in Belgium. They are also responsive to participatory input and keen to provide effective and efficient public service output. The chapter concludes that mayors could ensure the democratic anchorage of security-based interventions, but only if their solutions-focused intentionality can be overcome.

In 'Raising the flag: the state effects of public and private security providers at East Jerusalem's national parks', Lior Volinz examines the myriad ways in which public and private security providers perform the state and partake in a statecraft production of sovereignty. More specifically, the chapter explores the practices employed by public security actors and private security companies at the City of David/Wadi Hilweh national park in East Jerusalem. Volinz argues that the security provision at these spaces is not limited to the protection of the national parks' personnel, property and visitors, but is aimed rather at the performance of Israeli sovereignty in an occupied territory. Through the examination of a national park embroiled in national and ethnic contestation, he posits that daily practices employed by security agents contribute to the effort of crafting the state and reconfiguring its relations with different residents of the region. He argues that these different practices include 'showing presence', reassuring some residents while

10 *J. Peter Burgess* et al.

intimidating others and the deliberate enhancement of friction between security agents and local residents.

The concluding Part III of the book, 'Democratic control and ethical implications', opens with 'Evaluation and effectiveness of counter-terrorism' by Fiona de Londras. The chapter observes that in the past 15 years there has been an enormous expansion of counter-terrorism laws and policies at national, regional and international levels. Spurred on by the events of 9/11 and, later, the phenomenon of 'foreign terrorist fighters', states and international institutions have introduced laws and policies that encroach greatly on fundamental freedoms and human rights (at times in ways that undermine the democratic process), and the international conception of the 'rule of law' has been 'securitized' to a striking degree. What has been less common, however, is the comprehensive and reflexive evaluation of whether such measures are, in fact, effective. In this chapter, de Londras outlines this expansion in counter-terrorism and its impact on human rights, democracy and the rule of law in order to argue that an evaluation of effectiveness is key in maintaining the legitimacy of the counter-terrorist state and supra-state. The chapter then explores what the notion of 'effectiveness' means in this context, identifying both meta- and specific objectives as critical sites of analysis. Based on this, the chapter proposes key principles for the design of effectiveness evaluation, taking into account the particular challenges of evidence in the counter-terrorist context.

The book concludes with 'The bleak rituals of progress; or, if somebody offers you a socially responsible innovation in security, just say no' by Mark Neocleous. The chapter takes a stand against the idea that we should be searching for socially responsible innovations in security, taking as its starting point the way that security functions as an overwhelming power in modern society, justifying everything done in its name. The chapter seeks to connect this power to capital and the state more generally, arguing that the logic of security is to subsume everything it encounters, including developments in security which are thought of as 'socially responsible innovations'. The chapter argues that the idea of 'socially responsible innovations in security' is a means by which radicals and academics seek to assert some kind of influence in the social field, but which reveals what is in fact their complete powerlessness in the face of security (and therefore in the face of capital and the state). In seeking socially responsible innovations in security, the power of security is thereby confirmed rather than challenged. The chapter will therefore be an argument against the logic which underpins the rest of the chapters in the book.

References

Appleyard, R.T. and Stahl, C.W., 1995. *South Pacific migration: New Zealand experience and implications for Australia.* Canberra: Australian Agency for International Development.

Blok, V. and Lemmens, P., 2015. The emerging concept of responsible innovation: Three reasons why it is questionable and calls for a radical transformation of the concept of innovation. In: B.-J. Koops, I. Oosterlaken, H. Romijn, T. Swierstra and J. van den

Hoven, eds., *Responsible Innovation 2: Concepts, approaches, and applications*. Dordrecht: Springer International Publishing, pp. 19–35.

Bozeman, B., 2007. *Public values and public interest: Counterbalancing economic individualism*. Washington, DC: Georgetown University Press.

Bozeman, B. and Sarewitz, D., 2011. Public value mapping and science policy evaluation. *Minerva*, 49(1), pp. 1–23.

Davies, S.R., Glerup, C. and Horst, M., 2014. On being responsible: Multiplicity in responsible development. In: S. Arnaldi, A. Ferrari, P. Magaudda and F. Marin, eds., *Responsibility in nanotechnology development*. London: The International Library of Ethics, Law and Technology, pp. 143–159.

De Jong, I.M., Kupper, F. and Broerse, J., 2016. Inclusive deliberation and action in emerging RRI practices: The case of neuroimaging in security management. *Journal of Responsible Innovation*, 3(1), pp. 26–49.

De Saille, S. and Medvecky, F., 2016. Innovation for a steady state: A case for responsible stagnation. *Economy and Society*, 45(1), pp. 1–23.

European Commission, 2013. *Options for strengthening responsible research and innovation*. Brussels: European Commission, Directorate General for Research and Innovation.

European Commission, 2016. *Horizon 2020. Work Programme 2016–2017*. Brussels: European Commission.

Gardner, J. and Williams, C.V., 2015. Responsible research and innovation: A manifesto for empirical ethics? *Clinical Ethics*, 10(1–2), pp. 5–12.

Grinbaum, A. and Groves, C., 2013. What is 'responsible' about responsible innovation? Understanding the ethical issues. In: R. Owen, J. Bessant and M. Heintz, eds., *Responsible innovation: Managing the responsible emergence of science and innovation in society*. London: John Wiley & Sons, Ltd, pp. 119–142.

Owen, R., Macnaghten, P. and Stilgoe, J., 2012. Responsible research and innovation: from science in society to science for society, with society. *Science and Public Policy*, 39(6), pp. 751–760.

Pelle, S. and Reber, B., 2015. Responsible innovation in the light of moral responsibility. *Journal on Chain and Network Science*, 15(2), pp. 107–117.

Sholten, V.E. and van der Duin, P.A, 2015. Responsible innovation among academic spin-offs: How responsible practices help developing absorptive capacity. *Journal on Chain and Network Science*, 15(2), pp. 165–179.

Stahl, B.C., 2013. Responsible research and innovation: The role of privacy in an emerging framework. *Science and Public Policy*, 40(6), pp. 708–716.

Stilgoe, J., Owen, R. and Macnaghten, P., 2013. Developing a framework for responsible innovation. *Research Policy*, 42, pp. 1568–1580.

Taebi, B., Correljé, A., Cuppen, E., Dignum, M. and Pesch, U., 2014. Responsible innovation as an endorsement of public values: The need for interdisciplinary research. *Journal of Responsible Innovation*, 1(1), pp. 118–124.

Valdivia, W.D. and Guston, D.H., 2015. *Responsible innovation: A primer for policymakers*. Washington, DC: Centre for Technology Innovation at Brookings Institute.

Van Oudheusden, M., 2014. Where are the politics in responsible innovation? European governance, technology assessments and beyond. *Journal of Responsible Innovation*, 1(1), pp. 67–86.

von Schomberg, R., 2011. Introduction. In: R. von Schomberg, ed., *Towards responsible research and innovation in the information and communication technologies and security technologies fields*. Brussels: European Commission, Directorate General for Research and Innovation, pp. 7–16.

1 Danger, innovation, responsibility

Imagining future security

J. Peter Burgess

Introduction

Security research has intensified at a break-neck speed in the months and years since 11 September 2011, when terrorism became an agenda-setting, globalized phenomenon. The particularly European approach to this global challenge has, however, set itself apart. The master-narrative of security governance in Europe has since the early 2000s focused on the development of an autonomous European security industrial sector and a corresponding Europe-wide market for the industrial development of security technologies. Research and development in security technologies has flourished in the last decades, supported by the good will of an industrially oriented security research programme, and a robust palette of liberalizing initiatives for the new digital market. The common value supporting these initiatives is a reborn concept of security innovation. Through the instruments at its disposition, the European Commission has advanced an agenda where security, the well-being of peoples and property, has become virtually synonymous with security innovation. 'Security' has become a tag for security-industrial dominance in relation to potential security threats. In short, security does not simply benefit from innovation; it is innovation.

The overall set of issues addressed by this volume revolves in one way or another around the question of what innovation understood as a kind of security measure can be. A first-cut answer to this question would situate innovation in relation to our own history, to what has been and to what will be, to what has had value in the past, and to what we hope will or expect to have value in the future. It is the search for improvement, for a better future, better quality, better performance and better alignment with the values that we hold dear. Yet if this is innovation, then surely security innovation redoubles the complexity of the problem. This is because security and security governance are precisely about safeguarding those things.

In his recent book, *Innovation Contested: The Idea of Innovation over the Centuries*, Benoît Godin documents how in the European sixteenth and seventeenth centuries, innovation was widely regarded not as a virtue, but as an evil. An 'innovator', according to Godin, was considered a threat to the recalcitrant church doctrine, and 'innovation' was in some cases severely punished (Godin,

Danger, innovation, responsibility 13

2015, pp. 75–101). What was new, uncharted, unthought or unrealized was regarded as detrimental to doctrine, a challenge to orthodoxy, even an existential threat to the institution of the church as it stood.

Today, on the scene of contemporary security research, the notion of innovation is of course regarded with unmitigated enthusiasm or even fetishized.[1] Innovation, an idea deployed with uncritical eyes, is a traditional key to understanding and analysing modernity. This fascination with the New has changed little, even while a multifaceted awareness of the limits and pitfalls of the pursuit of modernity and the critique of the modern remains an object of fascination and an axis of value and privilege. We seldom hear bad news about innovation. Even when the umbrella concept 'modernity' is subjected to post-modern critical scrutiny and the scepticism it provokes, 'innovation' as an idea and as an ideology seems to be an uncritical success.

What we do notice, however, is that the idea of innovation generates a range of secondary or adjacent questions. These questions concern, on the one hand, the sources of innovation, its motivations and justifications, its aims and ambitions; and on the other hand, the actual impact innovation has, how it affects the processes which it is meant to innovate, how it affects the consumers and citizens touched by it, how it influences the scientific or commercial environments where it functions and the natural environments in which it is played out.

It is one subset of these questions that leads us to the idea of 'responsible innovation', and to the question of how best to govern innovation for the benefit of both society and research itself. 'Responsible innovation' – as a concept and political strategy – seeks to take account of the criticisms of modernity, to counter-claims linked to the environment, development, health, safety and security, and builds an infrastructure of ethical consideration.

Responsible innovation is thus both the name of a kind of modernity and the name of a normative project, a project to be realized, an impulse and proposition for change. On the one hand, it is an analytic tool, the specification of a subset of the modern project, of creating new knowledge and new practices in which commercial progress and economic modernization are key points of valorization. On the other hand, it is a campaign designed to reinvent the fading momentum of modernity. It is a strategy for addressing one of the many political criticisms of modernization, namely its indifference to morality, its disdain for spirituality, its pretence of superiority in relation to human values. While it is more or less clear that all of these criticisms are problematic in their own way, the project of responsible innovation suspends these issues and forges on autonomously.

Another, highly relevant, subset of the general modernization project is the considerable research, development and investment that have taken place in security and security research in the last decades. While responsible innovation comprises a set of principles that might very well be applied to any project of Western industrial development, few such projects hold the same force and political sway as security. No other subfield of industrial innovation offers the same promise, political impact or economic consequences as security research and development.

14 *J. Peter Burgess*

Even though it is clear that there are distinct similarities between industrial innovation in security and industrial innovation in other fields, the aim of this chapter is to argue that the focus on responsible innovation in security research and development is a very different kind of problem, more convoluted and complex than responsible innovation in general, requiring a different kind of analysis than what we have seen in recent scholarship and policy work on responsible innovation.

This is because security is not just any one consumer item among others. Security is not – despite what we see all around us – a product or a service that can be bought and sold in any simple way. Security in its essence is something wider and deeper. It is a phenomenon that stems from and dialogues with our deepest humanity, with our hopes and fears, our ambitions and anxieties. For this reason, responsible innovation in security research requires us to look more closely at the nature of security and its relation to research and innovation.

In this chapter, we begin by looking more closely at the new landscape of security in Europe, the new security threats perceived by Europeans. We then return to a more detailed analysis of the concept of innovation and its history in the European context, charting its transition from its origins towards the idea of 'responsible innovation' in European Union-supported research and development. We conclude by examining how security and responsible innovation both diverge and come together in the European Union's struggle to understand itself by understanding what is threatening it.

What is under threat when Europe is under threat?

The starting point of the analysis of the responsible innovation in security research is naturally the new security reality in Europe and the West. This new reality consists of a perception of a new set of threats and an amalgam of dangers large and small, personal and collective, that populate and shape our world, a kind of ambient landscape of unease. We sketch this new security landscape along three dimensions: (1) the nearly ubiquitous mass of threats, real and imagined, that forms the backdrop of our lives; (2) the changes brought about in our way of understanding security and insecurity; and (3) the political consequences of the powerful new discourse of security.

To judge by the words and actions of the general public, pundits and public officials, Europe is under threat. But this threat is of a new kind, with a new structure and new components.

For the last year or so, migration has become an object of security analysis. The international balance of peoples and their movement is now under intense scrutiny as the European Union scrambles to put in place a coherent immigration policy while at the same time developing new technologies of surveillance of individuals and new legal paradigms for the juridical control of populations.

This sense of threat and insecurity is, however, not restricted to popular experiences of migration. It also leaves its mark on research and policy formation in this area. Unfortunately, this association of migration with security dissuades critical

Danger, innovation, responsibility 15

scrutiny of policy formulation and practice even while it shows a certain disregard for widely held European values.

In Europe today, migration from the war-torn Middle East and developing regions of the world to Europe is widely experienced as a threat, revealing a profound feeling of insecurity, which translates into a wide variety of political consequences.

We often hear of the way in which migration can have a threatening impact on societies, how it can introduce economic competition and undermine job security for nationals, how it can be associated with particular health risks, how it can have implications for security where it involves criminal activities, how it can affect national identity, and how it can be associated with the rise of xenophobia and discrimination.

The concept of security has traditionally referred to the status of sovereign states in a closed international system. In this system, the state is assumed to be both the object of security and the primary provider of security. But today, a wide range of security threats, both new and traditional, confront Europe. According to many, new forms of nationalism, ethnic conflict and civil war, information technology, biological and chemical warfare, resource conflicts, pandemics, mass migrations, transnational terrorism, and environmental dangers challenge the limits of our ability to safeguard the values upon which European society is based.

The growing awareness of these new threats has brought about a change in the way we understand the very concept of security. Consequently, our understanding of the security landscape needs to be nuanced. First, attention needs to be drawn to the complex and composite nature of the state's security, complicating the assumption that the state can be understood as a simple object of security. Second, the importance of non-state objects of security needs to be better conceptualized; that is, security that is related to that of state security but not identical to it. These objects can be divided into two kinds: on the one hand, individuals and sub-state groups, and, on the other, trans-state entities.

Across this wide horizon of insecurity, two distinct features characterize perceived threats to security: they surpass the boundaries of the nation-state and they are interconnected through processes of globalization. No one state can manage the array of threats to its own security, and nor can any one state manage the threats to the security of its neighbours both inside and outside Europe. In the globalized setting, the challenge of maintaining security is no longer limited to the traditional foreign-policy and military tools of the nation-state. Since at least the mid-1990s, security and insecurity are no longer considered as conditioned only upon geopolitics and military strength, but on social, economic, environmental, moral and cultural issues.

There is therefore widespread disagreement today about what security is, what threats contribute to making us insecure and how one should best seek to enhance security through research and development, communication policy, legal instruments and practice on the ground. This contention forms the backdrop for innovation today. To the degree that this security reality is perceived

16   *J. Peter Burgess*

and understood as being new, it generates a perceived need for novel approaches to addressing the new reality. The novelty of the threat landscape obliges novelty in security measures. At the same time, the experience of novelty is part and parcel of an experience of the unknown, and with it, a notion of unease. Novelty as unease is the well-known affective negation of progress and the support of cultural conservatism. When, in addition, novelty comes in the form of danger, uncertain threat from unknown nefarious forces with unfamiliar motives, the unease of novelty intensifies. Popular openness, industrial optimism and financial bullishness towards innovative responses to the new security reality become enhanced in kind.

This dynamic intensifies the sense that Europe finds itself at a crossroads with respect to the principles, values, means and methods of security policy, and research and development. The considerable shift in the security landscape has not yet been met with a corresponding renewed reflection on how security research and development should be organized, the type of security research policy that should be implemented to guide it and what kind of political structures – and safeguards – are needed to support it.

Despite this indecision, the novelty of threats and the force of events have meant that more resources than ever before are being committed to security research and development, often with the wrong focus. Crucial decisions are being taken over what security innovation policies should be chosen, how they should be implemented, who should fund them and who should benefit from them, without sufficient understanding of the social, political, cultural, ethical and scientific environments that surround them. There is increasing concern at the political level over the methods and aims of security policy and security research, reflecting a fundamental lack of consensus about what security actually is, how it should best be provided and how security research can best contribute to it. Against this backdrop, in what terms should we understand and seek innovation in security research and development?

Responsible innovation in Europe

The idea of innovation as a virtue first took root in the nineteenth century when it was associated with the industrialization process, and was synonymous with 'invention'. Under the new doctrine of industrial progress, the invention of technical solutions to technical problems was regarded as indispensable.

It was around the turn of the twentieth century that something closer to our contemporary usage of the term 'innovation' came into circulation. In his classic analysis of capitalism, *Theory of Economic Development*, published in German in 1911 (first published in English in 1934), the Austrian economist Joseph P. Schumpeter famously differentiated between 'invention', understood as an act of intellectual creativity, and 'innovation', understood as the moment when invention is inserted into changes in a business model (Schumpeter, 2012 [1911]).

This basic distinction remains with us today. It is that distinction between the human, creative invention of something whose value is regarded as implicit, inherent, unconditional, unqualified, self-determined and indeed self-affirming,

Danger, innovation, responsibility 17

and the creation of something new through its insertion into a social and material process, a system, a context. In contrast to the idea of invention, which refers to the creation of something new and valuable, which can subsequently be integrated into some context where it can meet concrete needs, an innovation has no value before it meets the context of its use. In other words, it derives its value in part from the context in which it is useful.

As mentioned above, few seem to hold criticism of innovation; we don't often hear bad news about innovation. Critical response to the notion of innovation has been rare. On the contrary, innovation somehow encapsulates implicit goodness, rightness. It is the story of history flowing in one direction, rationality evolving in one direction, progress towards change and the novelty implied by change; leaving behind, interrupting, disrupting or even destroying the past (as in Schumpeter's famous formulation) is largely taken for granted. Even in the terms of 'responsible innovation', the rightness of the project of innovation is self-evident, and the task of research governance is to gently steer it on its course, correcting its navigational errors.

This coincides in part with the evangelical calling of modernity. In modernity's vision of both reality and human values, what is new is regarded as superior – more real, more true, more valuable. The new is accepted as unconditionally superior to the past. It is not by accident then that in this ideological environment the concept of Responsible Research and Innovation (RRI) has risen to prominence in the discourse of European Union research. The concept of RRI is not at its heart about responsibility – or research, or innovation. The core political thrust of RRI is a political need to reduce the distance between research – above all, research funding – and the perceived needs, wishes, interests and values of the European taxpayers who fund them.

In the European Commission's version of the concept of RRI, it is defined in terms of collaboration. A colourful 2012 brochure says:

> Responsible Research and Innovation means that societal actors work together during the whole research and innovation process in order to better align both the process and its outcomes, with the values, needs and expectations of European society.
>
> (European Union, 2012)

In this vision RRI consists of six keys:

1 Engagement of all society actors (researchers, industry, policy-makers and civil society) and their joint participation in the research and innovation process.
2 Gender equality, meaning that all actors – men and women – can participate.
3 Science education.
4 Ethics, expressed through the cheerful yet somewhat sinister slogan 'Do the right "think"' – advancing the notion that fundamental rights and high ethical standards must inform research.

18 *J. Peter Burgess*

5 Open access for all to research results.
6 Governance; bringing public engagement to decision-making about how research is carried out and on what (European Union, 2012).

Around the time the Commission was warming the public up to the new jargon of research and innovation, an Expert Group was appointed, headed by Jeroen van den Hoven, to prepare a report on the state-of-the-art of RRI in Europe. In its 2013 report the following year, the experts sharpen and nuance somewhat the Commission's earlier popularized definition of the year before, referring to the comprehensive approach of proceeding in research and innovation in ways that allow all stakeholders involved in the processes of research and innovation at an early stage (A) to obtain relevant knowledge on the consequences of the outcomes of their actions and on the range of options open to them; (B) to effectively evaluate both outcomes and options in terms of societal needs and moral values; and (C) to use these considerations (under A and B) as functional requirements for the design and development of new research, products and services (European Union, 2013).

In short, the report takes the concept of RRI as a point of departure for a comprehensive review of the options for inserting the policy into research and innovation practices, and the likely outcomes the policy would have.

Recalling Schumpeter's 1911 distinction between invention and innovation, we can see that the RRI presupposes that research will become innovation through its interaction with society. But the expert report makes it abundantly clear that RRI is itself also an innovation, in that everything depends on the political choices that are made when inserting it into society.

Important criticism of the notion of responsible innovation has emerged. Blok and Lemmens, for example, argue that the concept is in acute need of revision from no fewer than four perspectives: First, it represents only (and tacitly) technological innovation; second, it is primarily perceived from an economic perspective; third, it is assumed to be inherently good; and fourth, it presupposes a symmetry between those actors who assume the position of emitting moral claims and those actors who are the addressees of those claims (Blok and Lemmens, 2015). But we want to suggest another, quite significant problem that arises in the attempt to bring the idea and ideology of RRI to the field of security research.

Responsible innovation as a response to security challenges

There are two problems in applying the concept of RRI to security research and development. The first is that responsible innovation is already about security – or perhaps insecurity. The second is that security research projects innovation into a dangerous future, which complicates the inherent goodness of innovation.

The romance of security and innovation goes way back, at least in modern times. Historians tell us that before the modern age, security was more akin to peace of mind. It was a spiritual matter and a largely religious one. From around

Danger, innovation, responsibility 19

the Feudal period, society's need for a more objective security became visible, and with it the willingness to pay for security. The transition to modern times saw the transformation of security into a commodity. Today, in the post-post-Cold War setting, security is not only inseparable from industrial interests; it is entirely unthinkable without it. In our time, security has become industrialized. We look overwhelmingly to industrial innovation to give us solutions to security challenges. Societies put their trust in technology and in the hands of the industries that produce it.

Our society is understood as a liberal one. Historically, security has played a part in the evolution of the liberal market system and in the emergence, development and maintenance of the liberal society. But liberal society is fragile, as we know; even precarious. It's easily weakened or damaged. Remarkably, though, it is most often not weakened or damaged from outside, but from within, either by official, unofficial, legal or illegal acts. In this sense, providing security against threats to our liberal society, liberal economies and markets most often means providing security against what we are capable of doing to ourselves. Obviously, if we understand security as stability, then a certain stability of prices is necessary for the prosperity of businesses. The regular flow of resources, labour and raw materials is equally a question of security. Businesses also depend to some degree on the continuity of demand, which can be secure or insecure. It also concerns physical security, the rule of law and social harmony of the society in which businesses operate – and innovate.

At the same time, we can see the reverse relation: a certain kind of innovation is indispensable to security. The security and well-being of society are enhanced by the success of businesses. Job security is served by economic prosperity, tax revenues are increased, investment is improved and a certain economic security can be found in the knock-on effects of successful commerce.

Security serves innovation; innovation serves security.

But we see in the liberal market system another paradox when it comes to security: in a sense, we can't live with it and can't live without it. We can't live without security, of course, for the reasons just mentioned: it is the platform on which we carry out the business of everyday life. Security is an enclosure, a blanket on which we can live out our lives and do business. On the other hand, however, liberal society – and its innovative aspirations – nurtures a certain kind of insecurity. Uncertainty is the starting point of the Western free market system. The public and private interest rate – the cost of borrowing money – varies according to the real or perceived uncertainty of future value. Moneylenders lend money at higher rates in the face of greater uncertainty, commodity prices or higher consumer prices, all as a function of perceived or real uncertainty.

Not security but *insecurity* is the driving force for innovation in Western liberal societies. Enormous sectors of our economy solicit and serve, either directly or indirectly, the insecurity of individuals and groups. In terms of finance, but also industrial research and development, insecurity is big business.

The second challenge we meet when attempting to adapt the notion of RRI to the question of security is time itself and the way the security invokes danger in

20   *J. Peter Burgess*

time. Of course innovation is always involved in meeting future challenges, but security challenges are different insofar as they stem from an acute sense of danger. They are inseparable from fear: fear of the future. Security threats are threatening not because we know what to expect, but precisely because we don't entirely know what they consist of. They come at us from an unknown, dangerous and fearful future.

Whereas we can innovate to address what are called issues of safety – known dangers that can be addressed by concrete means – for example, measures to make automobiles safer, to make the workplace safer, etc. – security threats always contain an element of the undecidable, something that cannot be planned for, or cannot be adapted to.

In this sense, security happens in the future. We are insecure today about the unknown event which may become a reality tomorrow. Innovation is, of course, also about the future, but the path to a secure future is not one that leads from here to there in any simple way. It's a bumpy and crooked path that leads through the culturally determined hopes and fears of societies that find themselves faced with unknown dangers.

Like the discourse of 'security', the discourse of 'fear' has been nourished by the rise of trans-national terrorism, though it has now shifted to the issue of international migration.

This reflexion also reminds us of the degree to which the principles and institutions of innovation depend on the ability to plan on a certain kind of predictability. Insecurity disrupts and destabilizes this predictability.

The tools of innovation depend on an array of assumptions about the relationship between present and future, and on the continuity of paths available for connecting the two, both in logical and emotional terms. The motivations and outcomes – inputs and outputs – that RRI takes as its signposts are rattled and shaken by the need to take fear itself as its guiding star – as its dependent variable.

The increasingly mainstream response to this situation is the application of one or other precautionary principle. Such principles express the imperative to take action in the absence, or in advance, of knowledge of the kind necessary to adequately make an informed decision. Furthermore, the precautionary principle presumes that such a decision must be taken, and consequentially actions taken, on the grounds that not taking action will have greater negative consequences than taking action.

Innovation depends on continuity, predictability, knowability, planning, governing, etc. that are not guaranteed in security research in the same way as they might be in engineering or medicine.

Conclusion

Responsible research and innovation share one important thing with security research. They are both motivated by a quest to affirm and promote socially relevant values. For responsible innovation, this means the values of democracy, transparency, equality, rationality, access, good governance and engagement.

Danger, innovation, responsibility 21

Security research does not oppose these values, but often operates in a world where they are themselves under threat. Security research of course aims to affirm core social values like democracy, transparency, equality, etc., but for many and in many contexts, they are regarded as part of the problem.

Indeed, in the European Commission's own Security Industrial Strategy, these values play little or no role. In this setting, 'innovation' is a common term, but does not refer to the democratic virtues. Innovation in European industrial security means standardization, harmonization and hybridization of intellectual property rights in order to assure quicker and more orderly access to a high-potential security market (European Commission, 2012).

For responsible innovation, the field of security research seems to be the final frontier.

Note

1 A vast sociological literature has documented the modern fascination with newness and with the degree to which the history of the modern is, among other things, the history of the economic, moral and aesthetic glorification of innovation (Giddens, 1990, 1991; Appadurai, 1996; Beck, 1997; Bauman, 2000; Brennan, 2000).

References

Appadurai, A., 1996. *Modernity at large: Cultural dimensions of globalization.* Minneapolis, MN: University of Minnesota Press.

Bauman, Z., 2000. *Liquid modernity.* Cambridge: Polity Press.

Beck, U., 1997. *The reinvention of politics: Rethinking modernity in the global social order.* Cambridge: Polity Press.

Blok, V. and Lemmens, P., 2015. The emerging concept of responsible innovation: Three reasons why it is questionable and calls for a radical transformation of the concept of innovation. In: B.-J. Koops, I. Oosterlaken, H. Romijn, T. Swierstra and J. van den Hoven, eds., *Responsible innovation 2: Concepts, approaches, and applications.* Heidelberg: Springer International Publishing, pp. 19–35.

Brennan, T., 2000. *Exhausting modernity: Grounds for a new economy.* London, New York: Routledge.

European Commission, 2012. Security industrial policy action plan for an innovative and competitive security industry {SWD (2012) 233 final}. Brussels: European Commission.

European Union, 2012. *Responsible research and innovation: Europe's ability to respond to societal challenges.* Brussels: European Union Publications Office.

European Union, 2013. *Options for strengthening responsible research and innovation: Report of the expert group on the state of art in Europe on responsible research and innovation.* Luxembourg: European Commission, Director-General for Research and Innovation.

Giddens, A., 1990. *The consequences of modernity.* Cambridge: Polity Press.

Giddens, A., 1991. *Modernity and self-identity.* Cambridge: Polity Press.

Godin, B., 2015. *Innovation contested: The idea of innovation over the centuries.* London: Routledge.

Schumpeter, J.A., 2012 [1911]. *Theory of economic development.* New York: Transaction.

Part I

Security technology, public perception and acceptance

2 Drones – dull, dirty or dangerous?

The social construction of privacy and security technologies

Marc van Lieshout and Michael Friedewald

Introduction

The Western world has experienced brutal attacks on a number of capitals over the past 10 years (Madrid, London, Paris, Brussels). While the background of the attacks may differ in the sense that different groups of terrorists were responsible for these attacks (Al Qaida and IS), each attack gave rise to intensified discourses on the need to invest additional resources in identifying potential terrorists in order to prevent new attacks from happening. While some organizations point at the astonishing fact that terrorist attacks overall have caused far more casualties among the Muslim population than among the non-Muslim population in the West, the attacks were clearly considered an attack on Western norms and values and an attempt to cause panic in the Western population. Understandably, part of the discourse was directed at the need to be able to collect more and more relevant information on potential terrorists.

Commenting on this, some pointed at the fact that usually it is not so much the lack of information but more the abundance of information (in combination with failing exchanges of information among the law enforcement agencies and intelligence services) that causes problems for the timely identification of potential terrorists in Western airports and cities.

After an attack, the 'balance' between privacy and security appears to shift in the direction of sacrificing privacy in exchange for better security, and after some time the pendulum starts swinging back. We put the term 'balance' deliberately in quotation marks to indicate that this is a false representation of what is really at stake (Valkenburg, 2015). In a four-year research project we have been able to study the relationship between privacy and security in depth from a variety of perspectives. In the PRISMS project (Privacy and Security Mirrors), a number of renowned research institutes studied this relationship from a socio-technological, policy, legal, criminological and media perspective.[1] The project performed a pan-European survey in which European citizens were asked how they value privacy and security as a social norm and a social objective (van den Broek *et al.*, 2017). All results were brought together in a decision support system that supports decision makers in adopting a more nuanced perspective on the relationship between privacy and security as a design principle for novel surveillance systems (van Lieshout, van Veenstra and Barnard-Wills, 2015).

In this chapter we will focus on the way security and privacy are institutionally embedded and how they function as socio-technical concepts in the construction of novel security systems. To start with the first, the presentation of the relationship between privacy and security as a trade-off implicitly qualifies security and privacy as equally relevant concepts and norms. While this may be so when looking at it from the perspective of constitutionally relevant rights to be respected (we have a right to privacy as well as a right to security[2]), this is far less trivial when looking at the means that are offered to realize a secure or a privacy-respecting situation. It is precisely this intriguing difference between the ideological role(s) of privacy and security and the manner in which these norms are embedded in practice that formed part of the research we performed in PRISMS (van Schoonhoven, Roosendaal and Huijboom, 2014).

A second and equally interesting perspective we explored is the way privacy and security are *inscribed* in technologies that are considered to enhance privacy and/or security. For some technologies, it is obvious that they can enhance both security and privacy. Encryption technologies, for instance, may both secure communications and help to secure privacy as well. The dual role of encryption technologies is an obvious example of the ambiguous relationship between a technological system or artefact and its role or use in practice. While encryption may secure communications and as such help secure part of life, criminals and terrorists may at the same time use it to secure their communications.[3] Depending on the context of use, encryption may thus qualify as a security technology, a privacy technology or both. An in-depth evaluation of precisely what norms are used when constructing specific technologies helps us understand the way social norms and behaviours are manifested in specific designs and layouts of technologies. While common sense presumes technologies are what they are (a door is a door, and a safety belt is a safety belt), the social construction of technology presumes all technologies are intrinsically shaped by social norms and practices and vice versa: the social understanding of technologies is shaped by the technologies at hand (Bijker, 1987, 1995; Latour, 2000). A relevant perspective we have used is the *inscription* of social norms in technology. We have explored this process for the construction of several different technologies, and in this chapter we will focus on a technology that is relatively new: the drone.

We will start with a presentation of the research methodology in order to explore our first research question: What do European research programmes reveal about the relevance of privacy and security as research topics, their interrelationship and the institutional backing towards achieving objectives in privacy and security as social norms? We will present and discuss our findings based on an analysis of a number of European research programmes (focusing on the European Commission's 6th and 7th Framework Programmes for Research and Technological Development – referred to as FP6 and FP7). In the second part of the chapter we will present our research methodology for exploring the so-called mutual shaping perspective on society and technology

Drones – dull, dirty or dangerous? 27

in the case of the development of drones. We will then present our analysis of the socio-technical construction of drones. Finally, we will present our overall conclusions, integrating both approaches and perspectives.

Research methodology for exploring the relationship between privacy and security and their prominence in European research programmes

Privacy and security are multidimensional concepts. They relate to social norms and practices. They are both grounded in the European Charter of Fundamental Rights, though the concept of security is less elaborated in legal practice than the concept of privacy. Despite this, security is a more developed concept when looking at the European policy landscape. Over the past decades, a European perspective on security has evolved in a set of policy documents.[4] From an industrial perspective, a so-called security industrial complex became more prominent, referring to the merging of interests of industry with the political elite (Barnard-Wills, 2013).[5] We were interested to know whether something like a privacy industrial complex could be made visible as well. Our intuition was that this does not exist. And though it is not entirely absent when one googles these keywords in combination, the number of real hits is rather limited.[6] We thus decided to check the European industry and innovation agendas to see how research and innovation activities within the European Union would contain reference to either security or privacy. For this to be done soundly, we had to define the concepts of privacy and security in greater detail.

PRISMS used a rather broad approach towards privacy and security. Both concepts were elaborated in seven distinct dimensions. In security, we added cultural security, environmental security and radical uncertainty security as novel ideological inroads to security. Security in our approach is thought to consist of the following dimensions (Lagazio, 2012):

1   *Physical security:* concerned with physical measures designed to safeguard the physical characteristics and properties of systems, spaces, objects and human beings.
2   *Political security:* concerned with the protection of acquired rights, established institutions/structures and recognized policy choices.
3   *Socio-economic security:* concerned with economic measures designed to safeguard the economic system, its development and its impact on individuals.
4   *Cultural security:* concerned with measures designed to safeguard the permanence of traditional schemas of language, culture, associations, identity and religious practices.
5   *Environmental security:* concerned with measures designed to provide safety from environmental dangers caused by natural or human processes.
6   *Radical uncertainty security:* concerned with measures designed to provide safety from exceptional and rare violence/threats, which are not deliberately

inflicted by an external or internal agent, but can still threaten drastically to degrade the quality of life.

7   *Information security:* concerned with measures designed to protect information and information systems from unauthorized access, modification or disruption.

The concept of privacy has a long history and it has been defined in many ways. Back in 1890, Warren and Brandeis defined it as 'the right to be let alone' (Warren and Brandeis, 1890). In 1967, the influential privacy researcher Alan Westin described it as 'an instrument for achieving individual goals of self-realization' (Westin, 1967, p. 39) and 'the claim of individuals, groups or institutions to determine for themselves when, how and to what extent information about them is communicated to others' (Westin, 1967, p. 7). Agre and Rotenberg (1997, p. 3) provided a frequently used definition of privacy as being free from unreasonable constraints. This relates to the distinction made by Isaiah Berlin in a famous presentation in 1958 between positive and negative freedom, in which the negative part relates to 'being free from … [intrusion by others, unreasonable constraints]' and the positive part refers to 'being free to … [make choices, judgements and decisions about one's own destiny]' (Berlin, 1962, pp. 122ff.). Recently, a conceptualization of privacy as seven types of privacy has been suggested by Finn, Wright and Friedewald (2013). This approach has been used throughout the PRISMS project:

1   *Privacy of the body:* the right to keep body functions and body characteristics (such as genetic codes and biometrics) private.
2   *Privacy of behaviour:* the right to keep actions and behaviour private, including sensitive issues such as sexual preferences and habits, political activities and religious practices.
3   *Privacy of communication:* the right to avoid the interception of communications.
4   *Privacy of data and image:* the right to protection of an individual's data from being automatically available or accessible to other individuals and organizations and ensuring that people can exercise a substantial degree of control over that data and its use.
5   *Privacy of thoughts and feelings:* the right not to share thoughts or feelings or to have those thoughts or feelings revealed.
6   *Privacy of location and space:* the right to move about in public or semi-public space without being identified, tracked or monitored.
7   *Privacy of association:* the right to associate with whomever one wishes, without being monitored.

This is a very broad description that not only captures the four dimensions (privacy of the body, communications, data and images, and location and space) in the popular definition by Roger Clarke (2006) but also adds behaviour, thoughts, and feelings and associations. The first two of these relate to very personal aspects of one's personality while the third relates to an essential aspect of privacy that has a more collective notion: being able to gather with whom one wants.

Identifying the occurrence of privacy and security in European research activities

Having defined privacy and security as concepts, we had to relate them to the practices of security and privacy industrialists. We decided to perform a keyword analysis on European framework programmes for research and innovation. The keyword search was performed on three sets of keywords. The first analysis simply used the keywords 'privacy' and 'security'. The second set of keywords referred to the security missions defined by the European Union in its most recent policy programme on security: 'critical infrastructures', 'terrorism and organized crime', 'disaster management' and 'border security' (European Commission, 2012). The third set of keywords relate to capabilities that are key to many security applications and that strongly relate to privacy issues: 'detection', 'identification' and 'surveillance' were the most prominent. The corpus was created by performing a keyword check on all projects from FP5 (1998–2002), FP6 (2002–2007) and FP7 (2007–2013). The initial keyword check was to identify those projects that mentioned 'privacy' and/or 'security' in the objectives of the project description. This resulted in 413 FP5-projects, 505 FP6-projects and 1415 FP7-projects. Since FP7 lasted for seven years while FP6 and FP5 each lasted for four years, part of the growth of the number of projects in FP7 can be attributed to the longer duration of the research programme. But at first glance one can notice that the number of security- and/or privacy-related projects show a growth over the years studied (2000–2014).

Drivers and barriers

The second part of the analysis consisted in identifying the drivers of and barriers to privacy and security technologies. These drivers and barriers were identified on the basis of an analysis of policy documents (such as those that form the basis of the European Security Agenda), technology roadmaps, foresight studies and impact assessments.[7] As drivers we identified 'push from technology and industry'; 'events with a high social impact'; 'national and EU-level policy and regulation'; and 'citizen demand for security and/or privacy'. As barriers we identified 'security and privacy not being unique selling points', but usually part of a broader setting; 'lack of standardization'; and a 'reactive approach' towards implementing security and/or privacy technologies.

Privacy and security in EU research programmes

We first selected those projects of FP5, FP6 and FP7 that had 'privacy' and/or 'security' in their objective descriptions. This means that projects dealing with security building blocks but not mentioning 'security' in the objective description were left out. The number of projects found is thus a lower estimate of the total number of projects dealing with privacy and/or security issues (see Figure 2.1).

If we were to neglect the rather anomalous results for 2003 and 2007, we can observe a steady rise of projects in which either security or privacy plays a role. The lower contributions of 2003 and 2007 relate to the start of the new programme in that year and the ending of the previous one (end of FP5 and start of FP6 in 2003 and similar for FP6 and FP7 in 2007). The lower contributions of 2005 and 2009 are more difficult to explain. If we were to leave those out, we can observe that in the latter years (2012–2014) attention towards privacy and security seems to have stabilized. We also identified the presence of privacy and security in the full description of the projects (except for the objectives), where it shows that attention to security is roughly five times higher than attention to privacy, with some correction in the latter three years (going down to four times higher).

Second, in the created sample of projects with privacy and/or security in the objectives, we selected the number of projects in which reference was made in the project objective description to the security missions of the EU (i.e. critical infrastructures, terrorism and organized crime, disaster management, and border security). The results are plotted in Figure 2.2.

The figure shows that FP5 paid a lot of attention to critical infrastructures but hardly any to the other topics, while FP7 shows a much more equal spread over the various topics in its latter years. Terrorism, disaster management and border

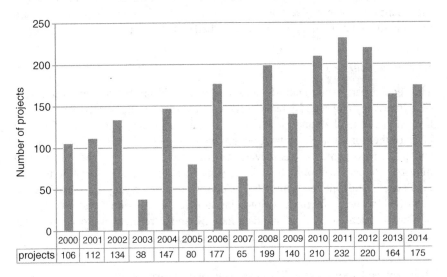

Figure 2.1 Number of projects from FP5, FP6 and FP7 with 'privacy' and/or 'security' mentioned in their objectives.

Source: van Schoonhoven, van Lieshout and Roosendaal, 2015, p. 39.

Drones – dull, dirty or dangerous? 31

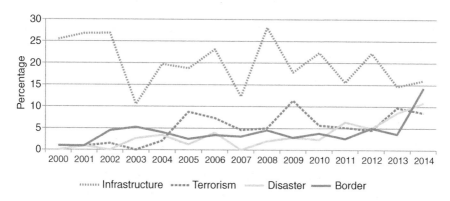

Figure 2.2 Relative keyword usage over time.
Source: van Schoonhoven, van Lieshout and Roosendaal, 2015, p. 40.

security received far more attention in the latter years than initially. The policy orientation of the EU towards covering these topics as part of the EU security agenda has had an impact on the relevance of these topics in research and innovation projects.

Third, we selected capabilities that are key to many security applications and that relate to potential infringements of privacy: *detection, identification* and *surveillance*. Figure 2.3 presents the results of the presence of these three terms in the project objectives.

The figure shows the rise of the keywords *detection* and *surveillance* over time, while the keyword *identification* gradually decreases. In absolute figures, one can notice that *surveillance* grows considerably between 2000 and 2014 (a fivefold increase), *detection* exhibits a threefold increase and *identification*

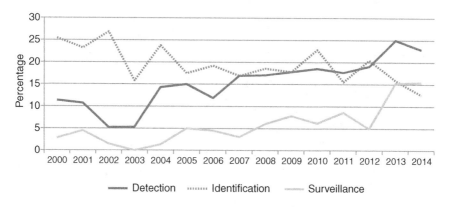

Figure 2.3 Relative keyword usage over time.
Source: van Schoonhoven, van Lieshout and Roosendaal, 2015, p. 41.

32 *Marc van Lieshout and Michael Friedewald*

remains more or less equal. The more in-depth investigation of the technology roadmaps revealed that the capabilities of the first two indeed become more mature and more interesting, while the capabilities for identification do grow as well but not as much as those of surveillance. The growing maturity of detection and surveillance technologies is supported by the attention they receive in research and innovation projects.

Drivers and barriers

Relevant drivers for investing in privacy and security technologies were identified on the basis of an analysis of roadmaps, foresights and policy documents (van Schoonhoven, Roosendaal and Huijboom, 2014). We checked the roadmaps, foresights and policy documents in arguments they provided for investing in security and/or privacy technologies. The result is presented in Table 2.1. The indicators should be considered as qualitative indicators that derive from a qualitative analysis of the roadmaps, foresights and policy documents we investigated.

The table shows that 'technology and industry push' act quite strongly in the field of security technologies but not as much in the field of privacy technologies. In this situation, whenever privacy technologies are promoted, it showed that this was because these technologies functioned to enhance both privacy and security (such as encryption technologies). Events with a high societal impact are shown to be quite relevant in promoting security technologies (a terrorist attack leading to increased acceptance of surveillance technologies, for instance), but less so for privacy technologies (a data breach, for instance, usually does not lead to a high demand for privacy technologies). One trivial explanation for this difference is the damage caused by a privacy infringement and a security infringement; one cannot hide away from a security incident (a terrorist attack or

Table 2.1 Factors driving and hindering technology development and use

	Factor	*Effect on technology development for security*	*Effect on technology development for privacy*
Drivers	Technology and industry push	Strong	Weak
	Events with high societal impact	Strong	Weak
	Government policy and regulation	Strong	Strong
Barriers	Consumer demand	Strong	Strong
	Lack of standardization	Strong	Strong
	Not a unique selling point	Average	Strong
	Reactive approach	Average	Strong

Source: van Schoonhoven, van Lieshout and Roosendaal, 2015, p. 8.

a natural disaster does not distinguish between victims), while a privacy incident may cause inconvenience for just a select group of people (those whose data were stolen or captured). The final two drivers offer strong incentives for both privacy and security technologies. In the case of privacy we should, however, be aware of the fact that at present, a strong consumer demand does not really exist.

The three identified barriers have also proven to be relevant for privacy technologies, while two of them are less relevant for security technologies. A lack of standardization is a problem for both privacy and security. Firms are very reluctant to advertise themselves as privacy proof since this may backfire on them the very moment they experience a privacy infringement. Moreover, most customers do not yet consider privacy to be a distinguishing feature, and thus would not value one specific security technology over another (London Economics, 2010; van Lieshout and Kool, 2012). At present, security and privacy are often added to a system after the completion of the functional design and implementation. This is changing, however, among other reasons because of recent European legislation that emphasizes the need to include privacy as an integral element in a system's design.[8]

The socio-technical construction of drones

The second part of our analysis focuses on the discourses related to the development of drones as exemplary security technology. Drones are a relatively recent technological innovation. Because of the miniaturization of chips, advanced sensor systems, high-speed data links and new materials enabling relatively cheap construction of light-weight flying vehicles, over the past years Unmanned Aerial Vehicles (UAVs) or Unmanned Aircraft Systems (UASs) have become more common place in civilian environments.[9] UASs have been defined as 'powered, aerial vehicles that do not carry a human operator' and that 'can fly autonomously or piloted remotely, can be expendable or recoverable, and can carry a lethal or non-lethal payload' (Bone and Bolkcom, 2003). Drones are well known because of their killing capacity and their use in annihilating specified targets. This military use has framed drones as killer devices. Their capacity to fly autonomously makes them useful for situations that are considered too dangerous or too difficult for long-term stay for human beings. This can be in places with high radiation (nuclear power plants), collapsed buildings, high-risk fires or heavily polluted areas. They have become more commonplace for crowd management and as instruments for law enforcement (speed control, but also drug trafficking and tracking of immigrants). Scenarios that represent high privacy risks are easily constructed, such as monitoring of crowds in combination with facial recognition techniques. When used in low-flying mode, the sensory sensitivity of UASs is sufficiently high to be of use for situations in which large groups of people crowd together such as festivals, football stadiums or demonstrations.

The social construction of technology

Our basic assumption is that one needs an in-depth study of the way meaning is attributed to innovations by relevant stakeholders to understand the practices in which these innovations are used. Normally, we take a given technological configuration for granted, as the result of a rational development process in which rational guidelines such as efficiency, cost-effectiveness and fit-for-purpose considerations have been followed to offer the best design of a specific innovation. The success of the design is built in during the design process itself, since one may expect the developers to have followed a rational process in making design choices. Studies of the history of the design process of technological innovations have, however, opened the so-called black box of innovation and demonstrated a vivid world inside this black box (Bijker, Hughes and Pinch, 1987; Esser, Fleischmann and Heimer, 1998; Strübing, 2005). Actors attribute meaning to developments and make choices that are based on a variety of arguments and presuppositions that guide the research, and the outcome reached has eventually gone through a number of stages before it materializes and solidifies.

In our approach to the development of UASs, we adopt the perspective sketched by the Social Construction of Technology or SCOT (Bijker, 1987; Bijker and Law, 1992). SCOT identifies *relevant social groups, interpretative flexibility* and *closure* as important conceptual notions to understand the processes in which an innovation is shaped (Bijker, 1995). Relevant social groups negotiate the meaning of an artefact under construction. They determine specific outcomes or directions that an innovation may enter.[10]

Relevant social groups may change over time. In the case of UASs, it is relevant that the original design was constructed under military considerations, in which an issue such as privacy is approached in a fundamentally different way than in a civilian context.[11] *Interpretative flexibility* means that relevant social groups may have different interpretations of what the innovation is about, and that even within one single relevant social group this interpretation may change over time. The *context of use* is a relevant determinant for how an innovation is interpreted.[12] In the case of a UAS, again the interpretation of being used in a military context as a life-saving device needs to compete with the interpretation of a drone as a killing device. Similarly, the interpretation of a UAS in a civilian context may vary considerably depending on the context of use (tracking drug smugglers versus spying on the neighbours). Finally, the concept of closure presumes that in the end the interpretation of an artefact reaches a state in which most (if not all) people attribute the same meaning to the artefact. This process of closure is, however, never finalized in the sense that it is always possible to reopen the discourse on the interpretation of an artefact or system.

The case: Unmanned Aerial Systems

UASs are systems consisting of a flying unit, usually equipped with some kind of payload. The flying unit requires a ground station and a communication and data link. It 'can be as small as an insect or as large as a charter flight' (Eick, 2009). UASs are often classified by weight (from less than 100 grams to five tons), range (from one kilometre to over 2000 kilometres), altitude (from less than 250 metres to 20 kilometres) and endurance (from less than 20 minutes to 48 hours of permanent flight) (Kornmeier, 2012, p. 13).[13] Shapes vary considerably: airplane-like fixed-wing designs and multi-rotor systems that can take off and land vertically are currently prevalent, and there are also other aerodynamic shapes.

Most systems are remotely piloted and monitored by flight operators (pilots), either within their line of sight or by long-distance data links. In many cases, only one additional evaluator is needed for interpreting payload (sensor) data. In other cases, up to 180 persons are needed for the operation. Essentially, all those involved in the operation are located at the ground station.[14] However, there are aircraft that can fly (semi-)autonomously, e.g. on the basis of sensor and collision avoidance systems, Global Positioning System (GPS) coordinates and/or routes calculated on the basis of data obtained through sensors during flight (Hing and Oh, 2009, p. 6). Additionally, some UASs also have the capability to operate as swarms. Units communicate with each other and are able to perform complex tasks together.

As aircraft platforms, UASs can be seen as payload carriers. Limited by size and weight, different payloads can be attached depending on the mission. In most civilian applications, it is likely that a standard, infrared or thermal camera will be attached to get a bird's-eye view. Surveillance missions often require additional signal intelligence hardware. Armed UASs in the context of law enforcement are sometimes considered, but are not typically in use yet (Homeland Security News Wire, 2011). Sometimes the data captured by the payload are processed on-board, e.g. to calculate the flight path. However, it is more common for the payload to transfer its data to the ground station. There, they can be processed directly – for example, by means of pattern recognition algorithms – or stored for future analysis – either by man or machine.

In terms of operational advantages, unmanned aircraft are ideal for use with regard to the deployment on demand of small-scale systems or the high range, altitude and, most importantly, endurance of larger systems. In addition, UASs are argued to be more economically advantageous than manned aircraft – though this applies mostly to small-scale systems.[15] These characteristics are advantageous in different mission scenarios, including border protection, law enforcement and surveillance, airborne sea patrol, search and rescue operations, scientific data collection (e.g. in hurricanes) or shooting film-footage. In general, in comparison to manned aircraft, UASs are typically deployed in dull, dirty or dangerous missions.

Research method

In studying the socio-technical practices that are basic to the development of UASs, we conducted desk research and ten interviews with UAS operators, developers, manufacturers and researchers. The interviews were semi-structured (topic list) and were done by telephone, except for one (which was done face to face). The interviews were focused on getting to know the context of the research, development and deployment of UASs and the interpretations provided by the interviewees for specific design and deployment choices. In these choices, we focused especially on the role played by privacy and security. We interviewed five developers and/or manufacturers, one researcher and four users (of which two were potential users). The desk research included a review of academic literature, press coverage, corporate communication and websites, and material from watchdog groups and other societal organizations. Freedom of information requests regarding privacy impact assessments related to UASs were sent to police forces in Essex, Merseyside, Staffordshire and Derbyshire in the United Kingdom and to the police in North Rhine-Westphalia and the Federal Police in Germany (see Braun, Friedewald and Valkenburg, 2015, for further details).

Understanding privacy and security in drones

Privacy as defined by the PRISMS team is made up of several dimensions (see section on research methodology). Obviously, there is a relationship between the privacy of location and space and the reconnaissance opportunities provided by UASs. Persons need to be identified in some manner in order to track them. The interviewees indicated that such tracking has hardly occurred until now.

Whenever a UAS is used for issues such as crowd control, persons are identified on the basis of particular characteristics such as clothing they wear. Facial recognition is not a feature that is part of UASs at this point in time. Given progress made in camera technology, one would expect facial recognition to become more widespread as a feature of UASs in due time. The observation of persons without permission or in situations which people would find embarrassing, however, is an example of how UASs can intrude into the private life of individuals.

In contrast, neither developers nor users of UASs considered privacy to be a relevant design parameter, in the sense that technological measures could or should be taken in the design of the UASs to prevent the privacy of observed persons being violated. When asked, developers showed a legalistic interpretation of privacy which was equated to the legal obligations stemming from data-processing regulations. They did not deny the relevance of privacy as a feature or social norm to be respected; they simply did not consider a relationship between the technical design of the UAS and the legally enforced privacy requirements. This became visible in three distinct manners. First, developers did not consider themselves morally responsible for privacy issues. They considered this to be on the side of the users. The reliance on procedural mechanisms to solve privacy rather than inserting technical precautionary measures was a second feature shared among developers and users.

Third, both users and developers pointed to the supervisory authorities as the ones responsible for the legal framework to be abided by in issues of security.

Interestingly, the authorities mentioned were the aeronautical authority and the authorities that grant flight clearances, rather than the data protection authorities. By referring to the role of authorities, users and developers made clear that privacy was a mere matter of compliance, and – again – not a social norm to be realized. Finally, privacy was not considered a problem – yet. The prototypes under construction were not thought to deliver privacy problems, since these would not be used in circumstances that might expose or identify individual persons in privacy-invasive manners. This was reflected in the feedback provided by the freedom of information requests. Neither the UK officials nor the German officials indicated that they had any information to share on a privacy impact assessment (PIA). A PIA was not performed, since it was not legally required.[16]

Security is defined in the PRISMS project as consisting of several dimensions as well (see section on research methodology). Physical security and data security seem to be obvious candidates for UASs, though for different reasons. Data security is essential for the proper functioning of the communication of the flying object with the ground station and for the transfer of sensory data (images, heat patterns, spectral analysis). Physical security could be one of the objectives to be achieved by the UAS. It could be safeguarding individuals in difficult situations (disaster management, for instance), or tracking groups of individuals in order to manage crowds. Socio-economic security is also in reach of UASs, for instance when UASs are used to check pipelines in isolated or hard-to-reach areas.

The interviewees did not recognize physical security as an asset of UASs. Of course, they acknowledged that UASs could be used to achieve physical security, but they did not perceive this as an essential ingredient of the design process. This view was shared by developers and users. Similarly, offering socio-economic security was seen as an external objective to be realized and fully dependent on the precise use of the UAS. Data security was seen as a relevant parameter, for the reasons stated above. Contrary to the notion of security, both developers and users emphasized the role of safety as a design parameter.[17] UASs should function safely and predictably, potential malfunctions should be anticipated as much as possible and their remedies should be incorporated in systems design. Safety was a much stronger concern than security. This is a strong indication of the role responsibility of designers and users. Failures of UASs in ordinary situations would make the firms offering the UAS liable. Next to this legalistic interpretation (which offers strong grounds for including safety measures in the design), designers and users considered themselves to be morally responsible for flying UASs safely (for instance, when used to monitor crowds).

Conclusions from the case study

In summary, we can conclude from this case study that relevant social groups indeed determine the design process by inserting specific design parameters that relate to how they interpret their role and the role of the technology under construction. We identified developers, (potential) users and supervisory authorities to be relevant social groups. The ordinary public is not a relevant social group yet. The interpretation of privacy in the design process is legalistic, with supervisory authorities in the field of avionics and not in the field of data protection. Users accept moral responsibility for having a privacy-respecting approach. In the present applications, however, the technology is either not sophisticated enough or not applied in ways that invade the privacy of individuals, according to the users. This may change over time. Security is hardly considered a design parameter, though both designers and users acknowledge the relevance of security as an objective to be achieved by using UASs. Safety is the predominant interpretation held by users and developers, and again the most relevant argument to do so is because they want to avoid being liable in incidents. Finally, though not included as such in the case study in full, we want to conclude that closure is still far away for the meaning attributed to UASs. The ongoing development and sophistication of UASs, and the fact that UASs can be affordable for anyone interested in such novelties, will in our view cause concerns that may trickle back to designers of the UAS. The technical opportunities to include privacy in the design might be enforced by extending the circle of relevant social groups with data protection authorities and new legal frameworks such as the General Data Protection Regulation, which may enforce technical measures to promote privacy.

General conclusions

The first part of our analysis shows that security is more prominent than privacy, that a spread over security objectives can be observed that follows the European security policy and that surveillance becomes more prominent over the years. On the basis of desk research, we concluded that security has more drivers than privacy and privacy has more barriers than security. These drivers and barriers and the differences found in the keyword analysis lend credibility to the claim that the institutional setting of security is more advanced than the institutional setting of privacy. Essentially, while the security/surveillance industrial complex is blossoming and has resulted in political embeddedness through participation in the European security policy agenda, a similar privacy industrial complex cannot be identified.

In the subsequent case we presented (being one of six cases we studied in PRISMS), we explored in more detail how security and privacy are socially constructed in the technological design of Unmanned Aerial Systems (drones). We concluded that neither privacy nor security were adopted as guiding principles for the design of UASs, and that if any perspective prevailed by designers and users in this respect it is a legalistic perspective, oriented towards avoiding liability claims. With respect to privacy, we conclude that one relevant social group (the public at large) plays as yet no role at all in the design of UASs. While this is understandable considering that UASs were initially targeted for use on the military battlefield and have only relatively recently entered the civilian market, we expect that privacy as a design parameter may grow in influence over the coming years. Similarly, we fully acknowledge that security is a leading objective in the use of UASs, but this does not mean that security is part of the design process as such. Safety is a relevant guideline, again from a liability perspective. Safety will continue to play a relevant role in the development of UASs, since the use of UASs is expected to increase in civilian circles.

Notes

1 This work was carried out under the project 'PRISMS: Privacy and Security Mirrors', co-funded by the European Union's Seventh Framework Programme for research, technological development and demonstration under grant agreement 285399. For more information see: https://cordis.europa.eu/project/rcn/102282_en.html.
2 Article 7 of the European Charter of Fundamental Rights stipulates the right to private and family life, the home and communications, while article 6 stipulates the right to liberty and security of the person. While the right to liberty is elaborated in the restriction of this right when in detention or when requesting asylum etc., the right to security is much less elaborated. The Dutch constitution, for instance, lacks the identification of this right, an issue that has been discussed in several instances but has not yet led to any change in the constitution. A relevant argument brought forward is that of course the government is responsible for making the lives of its citizens safe, an obligation which is laid down in several other legal requirements such as securing public order. The German constitution does not mention a right to security either. Even more problematic, other constitutions and e.g. the UN charter of human rights mention the right to personal security fading out other types of security. See the presentation by Charles Raab at the Annual Privacy Forum: http://2015.privacyforum.eu/programme/presentation-raab.
3 The case of Apple against the FBI is a good example. Apple argues that it wants to make the messages of its client secure and that it does not want to offer a portal to the intelligence services that may help the services to identify criminals and terrorists, while the FBI wants the opportunity to be able to check and inventory communications when someone is under suspicion of criminal or terrorist intentions. www.wired.com/2016/02/apple-fbi-privacy-security (visited April 15, 2016).
4 We will not present the policy programmes in detail. Basically, what one can discern is an increase in complexity in topics covered (from more targeted objectives such as criminality and terrorism to a broader array of topics covering, for instance, ecological threats as well), and a simultaneous development in a broader array of technologies and technological systems, culminating in a 'systems of systems' approach in the latest security technology programme (see European Commission and Council of the European Union, 2003; ESRAB (European Security Research Advisory Board), 2006; European Security Research and Innovation Forum (ESRIF), 2009; European Commission, 2009, 2010, 2012).
5 The first high-ranked public official to mention the military industrial complex was Dwight Eisenhower in his famous farewell speech as president of the United States on January 17, 1961. Since then, the military industrial complex has evolved into a security industrial complex, with a focus not exclusively on military threats but on a much broader array of security threats (Milles, 2004; Hayes, 2009; Harris, 2011).
6 Though not scientifically sound, only two hits can be found on the first five pages when using Google. The most relevant hit refers to a 2012 conference on privacy identity innovation (Adler, 2012), while the second hit only bears privacy-industrial complex in its title. The same keywords score 18 links to the military industrial complex or the surveillance industrial complex on the same five pages.
7 For a complete overview of the consulted documents see van Lieshout et al. (2015, Appendix B).

8 The new European General Data Protection Regulation (accepted April 14, 2016) enforces privacy by design (article 25).

9 To the degree that they are within easy reach of hobbyists. For hobby uses, specific rules and regulations apply, such as Line of Sight flight plans and keeping objects under specific height levels (in which other aerial objects are present as well) (Finn and Wright, 2012).

10 A famous case study demonstrating the relevance of these social groups is the construction of the bicycle. Bijker (1995) demonstrates how the original bicycle was constructed as a 'macho' bike (with high wooden wheels) that was unfit for use by women, and that only after several decades was the bicycle shaped as we know it today, including all kinds of partial innovations such as inflatable tires and a chain for ease of biking. Today, new innovations re-open the presumed closure of the bicycle, for instance by adding electrical power to bicycles.

11 In situations of life-threatening dangers, the privacy of the soldiers at the battlefield is less an issue to reckon with. This does not imply that privacy is not an issue at all, but – depending on the context of use – it will be less relevant when designing a UAS to be of help on the battlefield.

12 Safety belts and the safety construction of a car were considered to make driving a safer exercise. On the other hand, it led to less careful driving, since the car was safe. The interpretation of the safety belt changed from perceiving the safety belt as a life-saving device to a device that enabled speeding and reckless driving.

13 By contrast, manned helicopters owned by the federal police force in Germany have a time of flight of up to 4.5 hours. See www.bundespolizei.de/DE/06Die-Bundespolizei/ Ausstattung/Hubschrauber/hubschrauber_node.html, visited July 23, 2013).

14 The number of operators depends on a system's size. Only one person is needed to operate a very small UAS. In contrast, it is said that a huge fixed-wing model, the MQ-9 Reaper by Northrup Grumman, requires more than 180 people to operate it (*Economist*, 2011).

15 See Kornmeier (2012, p. 8). Accordingly, small-scale systems mostly have low range, altitude and endurance. Large and mostly fixed-wing UASs having a high range, altitude and endurance are generally very expensive. For example, the Global Hawk by Northrop Grumman, which is not yet in use for civil applications, costs about $222 million without maintenance costs. In addition, one interviewee stated that because of personnel and infrastructure costs, an unmanned flight is generally more expensive than manned flights, except for systems that can be operated by few persons (see GAO (Government Accountability Office) and Koontz, 2007, p. 113).

16 In Europe, Privacy Impact Assessments are a relatively new instrument (see Wadhwa and Rodrigues, 2013). A 'data protection impact assessment' is an instrument foreseen by the new European Data Protection regulation (Regulation (EU) 2016/679, Art. 25).

17 All interviewees were German-speaking. In German there is just one single word to indicate security and safety: 'Sicherheit'. We inferred the distinct notions of Sicherheit as referring either to 'security' or to 'safety' from the context of usage.

References

Adler, J., 2012. #pii2012: the emergent privacy-industrial complex [online]. Available at: https://jimadler.me/pii2012-the-emergent-privacy-industrial-complex-dd274f0523f [accessed June 26, 2017].

Agre, P.E. and Rotenberg, M., 1997. *Technology and privacy: the new landscape*. Cambridge, MA: MIT Press.

Barnard-Wills, D., 2013. Security, privacy and surveillance in European policy documents. *International Data Privacy Law*, 3(3), pp. 170–180.

Drones – dull, dirty or dangerous? 41

Berlin, I., 1962. *Four essays on liberty*. Oxford: Oxford University Press.

Bijker, W.E., 1987. The social construction of bakelite: toward a theory of invention. In: W. Bijker, T.P. Hughes and T. Pinch, eds., *The social construction of technological systems: new directions in the sociology and history of technology*. Cambridge, MA: MIT Press, pp. 159–187.

Bijker, W.E., 1995. *Of bicycles, bakelites, and bulbs: toward a theory of sociotechnical change*. Cambridge, MA: MIT Press.

Bijker, W.E. and Law, J., 1992. *Shaping technology/building society: studies in socio-technical change*. Cambridge, MA: MIT Press.

Bijker, W.E., Hughes, T.P. and Pinch, T.J. eds., 1987. *The social construction of techno-logical systems: new directions in the sociology and history of technology*. Cambridge, MA: MIT Press.

Bone, E. and Bolkcom, C., 2003. *Unmanned aerial vehicles: background and issues for congress* [pdf]. Washington, DC: Congressional Research Service. Available at: www.fas.org/irp/crs/RL31872.pdf [accessed June 26, 2017].

Braun, S., Friedewald, M. and Valkenburg, G., 2015. Civilizing drones: military dis-courses going civil. *Science & Technology Studies*, 28(2), pp. 73–87. Available at: http://ojs.tsv.fi/index.php/sts/article/view/55351 [accessed June 26, 2017].

Clarke, R., 2006. What's 'privacy'? In: Australian Government, *Australian Law Reform Commission Workshop*. July 28, 2006. Available at: www.rogerclarke.com/DV/Privacy.html [accessed June 26, 2017].

Economist, 2011. Flight of the drones: why the future of air power belongs to unmanned systems. *The Economist* [online], October 8. Available at: www.economist.com/node/21531433 [accessed June 26, 2017].

Eick, V., 2009. Das Dröhnen der Drohnen: Technisierung von Überwachung und Kon-trolle. *Bürgerrechte und Polizei/CILIP*, 94(3/2009), pp. 28–40.

ESRAB (European Security Research Advisory Board), 2006. *Meeting the challenge: the European security research agenda. A report from the European Security Research Advisory Board* [pdf]. Luxembourg: Office for Official Publications of the European Communities. Available at: www.kowi.de/Portaldata/2/Resources/fp7/coop/security-esrab-report-2006.pdf [accessed June 26, 2017].

Esser, J., Fleischmann, G. and Heimer, T. eds., 1998. *Soziale Schließung im Prozeß der Technologieentwicklung*. Frankfurt, New York: Campus.

European Commission, 2009. *A European security research and innovation agenda – Commission's initial position on ESRIF's key findings and recommendations*. COM (2009) 691 final, Brussels. Available at: http://ec.europa.eu/dgs/home-affairs/e-library/documents/policies/security/pdf/comm_pdf_com_2009_0691_f_communication_en.pdf [accessed June 26, 2017].

European Commission, 2010. *The EU internal security strategy in action: five steps towards a more secure Europe*, COM (2010) 673 final, Brussels. Available at: http://eur-lex.europa.eu/legal-content/EN/TXT/PDF/?uri=CELEX:52010DC0673&from=EN [accessed June 26, 2017].

European Commission, 2012. *Security industrial policy: action plan for an innovative and competitive security industry*, COM (2012) 417 final, Brussels. Available at: http://eur-lex.europa.eu/LexUriServ/LexUriServ.do?uri=COM:2012:0417:FIN:EN:PDF [accessed June 26, 2017].

European Commission and Council of the European Union, 2003. *A secure Europe in a better world – European security strategy*. Brussels. Available at: www.consilium.europa.eu/uedocs/cmsUpload/78367.pdf [accessed June 26, 2017].

42 Marc van Lieshout and Michael Friedewald

European Security Research and Innovation Forum (ESRIF), 2009. *ESRIF final report*, Ares(2014)74540, Brussels. Available at: http://ec.europa.eu/DocsRoom/documents/1413/attachments/1/translations/en/renditions/pdf [accessed June 26, 2017].

Finn, R.L. and Wright, D., 2012. Unmanned aircraft systems: surveillance, ethics and privacy in civil applications. *Computer Law & Security Review*, 28(2), pp. 184–194.

Finn, R.L., Wright, D. and Friedewald, M., 2013. Seven types of privacy. In: S. Gutwirth, R. Leenes, P. De Hert and Y. Poullet, eds., *European data protection: coming of age*. Dordrecht: Springer, pp. 3–32.

GAO (Government Accountability Office) and Koontz, L.D., 2007. *Homeland security: continuing attention to privacy concerns is needed as programs are developed* (GAO-07-630T) [pdf]. Washington, DC: United States Government Accountability Office. Available at: www.gao.gov/new.items/d05866.pdf [accessed June 26, 2017].

Harris, P., 2011. How private firms have cashed in on the climate of fear since 9/11. *Guardian* [online]. September 5. Available at: www.guardian.co.uk/world/2011/sep/05/private-firms-fear-9-11 [accessed June 26, 2017].

Hayes, B., 2009. *NeoConOpticon: the EU security-industrial complex*. Amsterdam: Transnational Institute. Available at: www.statewatch.org/analyses/neoconopticon-report.pdf [accessed June 2, 2017].

Hing, J.T. and Oh, P.Y., 2009. Development of an unmanned aerial vehicle piloting system with integrated motion cueing for training and pilot evaluation. In: K.P. Valavanis, P. Oh and L.A. Piegl, eds., *Unmanned aircraft systems*. Dordrecht: Springer, pp. 3–19.

Homeland Security News Wire, 2011. Texas county police buys drone that can carry weapons. *Homeland Security News Wire* [online], October 31. Available at: www.homelandsecuritynewswire.com/texas-county-police-buys-drone-can-carry-weapons [accessed June 26, 2017].

Kornmeier, C., 2012. *Der Einsatz von Drohnen zur Bildaufnahme: Eine luftverkehrsrechtliche und datenschutzrechtliche Betrachtung*. Münster: Lit Verlag.

Lagazio, M., 2012. The evolution of the concept of security. *The Thinker*, 43(9), pp. 36–43.

Latour, B., 2000. The Berlin key or how to do words with things. In: P.M. Graves-Brown, ed., *Matter, materiality and modern culture*. London: Routledge, pp. 10–21.

London Economics, 2010. *Study on the economic benefits of privacy-enhancing technologies (PETs)* [online]. London: London Economics. Available at: http://ec.europa.eu/justice/policies/privacy/docs/studies/final_report_pets_16_07_10_en.pdf [accessed June 26, 2017].

Milles, M., 2004. The security-industrial complex. *Forbes* [online]. Available at: www.forbes.com/forbes/2004/1129/044.html [accessed June 26, 2017].

Strübing, J., 2005. *Pragmatistische Wissenschafts- und Technikforschung: Theorie und Methode*. Frankfurt, New York: Campus.

Valkenburg, G., 2015. Privacy versus security: problems and possibilities for the trade-off model. In: S. Gutwirth, R. Leenes and P. De Hert, eds., *Reforming European data protection law*. Dordrecht: Springer, pp. 253–269.

van den Broek, T., Ooms, M., Friedewald, M., van Lieshout, M. and Rung, S., 2017. Privacy and security: citizens' desire for an equal footing. In: M. Friedewald, J.P. Burgess, J. Cas, R. Bellanova and W. Peissl, eds., *Surveillance, privacy and security: citizens' perspectives*. London: Routledge, pp. 15–35.

van Lieshout, M. and Kool, L., 2012. *Designing privacy: motivating and hindering factors for Dutch companies*. Amsterdam Privacy Conference. The Netherlands, Amsterdam, October 7–10, 2012.

van Lieshout, M., van Schoonhoven, B., Roosendaal, A., Valkenburg, G., Huijboom, N., van Veenstra, A.F., Braun, S. and Friedewald, M., 2015. *PRISMS Deliverable 2.3: Security and privacy technologies: understanding trends and developments* [pdf]. Available at: http://publica.fraunhofer.de/eprints/urn_nbn_de_0011-n-3674295.pdf [accessed June 26, 2017].

van Lieshout, M., Barnard-Wills, D., Friedewald, M. and González Fuster, G., 2015. *Deliverable 11.3: The PRISMS decision support system.* Available at: http://publica.fraunhofer.de/documents/N-349845.html [accessed March 13, 2018].

van Schoonhoven, B., Roosendaal, A. and Huijboom, N., 2014. Privacy versus collective security: drivers and barriers behind a trade-off. In: M. Hansen, J.-H. Hoepman, R. Leenes and D. Whitehouse, eds., *Privacy and identity 2014, IFIP AICT, vol. 421.* Heidelberg, Berlin: Springer, pp. 93–101.

van Schoonhoven, B., van Lieshout, M. and Roosendaal, A., 2015. *Deliverable 2.3: Security and privacy technologies: understanding trends and developments – Part A.* Available at: http://publica.fraunhofer.de/documents/N-367429.html [accessed March 13, 2018].

Wadhwa, K. and Rodrigues, R., 2013. Evaluating privacy impact assessments. *Innovation: The European Journal of Social Science Research*, 26(1–2), pp. 161–180.

Warren, S.D. and Brandeis, L.D., 1890. The right to privacy. *Harvard Law Review*, 4(5), pp. 193–220.

Westin, A.F., 1967. *Privacy and freedom.* New York: Atheneum.

3 The influence of technological innovations on theft prevention

Perspectives of citizens and experts

Kim Van Hoorde, Evelien De Pauw,
Hans Vermeersch and Wim Hardyns

Introduction

Promising to transform the way we live, work and communicate, the emergence of the 'Internet of Things' (IoT) is an important topic of study with a clear technical, social and economic significance (Rose, Eldridge and Chapin, 2015). The IoT refers to everyday objects that have the ability to connect to the Internet, each other and the environment to produce, store, transmit and communicate information and data (FTC, 2015). At the end of the first decade of this century, the world had reached an Internet milestone. Consumer products, goods, cars, sensors, other everyday objects and even houses are now being combined with Internet connectivity and data analytic capabilities, leading to numerous new applications and possibilities.

Technological innovations, however, facilitate not only social development, but also crime (Ekblom, 2005). The use of technological systems related to the IoT may represent new challenges towards criminals and may influence their selection of targets, as well as their probability of success. According to critics, crime can be controlled, but rarely 'eradicated', and the use of new technologies in control strategies is often only partially effective and tends to become less effective over time (Ekblom, 2005; Nuth, 2008). Moreover, new technologies that facilitate crime control may accelerate the crime rate: technology innovations trigger new innovations, often as a counter-mechanism to the previous one. Increasingly, criminals do not have to be physically present at a scene to pursue crime, as they can operate from a remote location over the Internet (Nuth, 2008). As such, the IoT may present a new, virtual door to buildings.

In the 'battle' against domestic burglary, several technological systems can be implemented as measures of prevention. In the near future, it is estimated that about 90 million people, globally, will use technology to improve home comfort and energy usage, for example, but also to secure their homes and property (Jacobsson, Boldt and Carlsson, 2016). Technological developments, however, have taken such a flight that society hardly has the time to examine their effectiveness, to regulate their use or to analyse their potential and unintended consequences. New technologies are often implemented without the presence of evidence-based research and when implementing them, there are some pitfalls to be taken into account (Corbett and Marx, 1991; Nuth, 2008). Moreover, techno-logical innovation has the potential to improve both the efficiency and the effec-tiveness of crime control, but it also has the potential to divert critical resources away from more traditional crime prevention strategies that may actually keep our houses safer. Organizational and construction-related prevention measures[1] do not suffer from the same potential negative side effects that come with tech-nology and the Internet (electronic measures), i.e. hackers could open a digital back door if they get inside your network, and thus get inside your home (Byrne and Marx, 2011).

As houses will be increasingly computerized and filled with devices in the near future, ranging from smart TVs to safety surveillance cameras, potential computer security breaches and their impact on residents need to be investigated. Combined, these applications that are typically developed for other (non-security related) purposes bear the potential to undermine the user's privacy and thereby jeopardize home security in ways that are difficult to predict (Jacobsson, Boldt and Carlsson, 2016). Evaluation of technology strengths and weaknesses should start with the perspective of the subjects that are bearing the costs and the implications of security policies: the citizens as individual users (Pavone, Esposti and Santiago, 2013). While the public may be ready to welcome new technolo-gies into their lives, they may not be readily equipped with the know-how regarding handling these innovations and dealing with the unintended con-sequences and/or securing them to ensure that their personal (online) data remain safe.

This research track is part of a larger project that aims at understanding new upcoming technologies and how they influence theft prevention, more specifi-cally domestic burglary, currently and in the near future.[2] To narrow the broad domain of new upcoming technologies, this project focuses on three specific systems: (1) home automation, (2) access control through biometric authentica-tion and (3) track and trace of objects. The project specifically reports on an explorative study on the use of the aforementioned new technologies by gather-ing useful information about how citizens use them as prevention measures with regard to domestic burglary.

A healthy level of self-sufficiency and a good information position are required to give citizens an active role in theft prevention and the fight against burglary. The knowledge, perspectives and experiences of citizens are critical for understanding and responding to their needs when it comes to the application of electronic measures with regard to domestic burglary. As such, this study wants to develop a better understanding of technology systems in order to antici-pate and coordinate the current prevention policy to it.

Research objectives and methodology

The goal of this study was to examine the efficient use of the aforementioned technological systems by:

46 *Kim Van Hoorde* et al.

i the identification of security questions and threats to the fundamental crime prevention measures in the fight against domestic burglary, more specifically with regard to the use of (1) home automation systems, (2) biometrics and (3) track-and-trace systems;

ii making an inventory of the practical information concerning the technical, legal and privacy issues concerning the use of those three technologies to prevent burglary;

iii mapping the perceptions and expectations of citizens in relation to those technologies; and

iv building an information base in order to formulate evidence-based techno prevention advice towards citizens.

To achieve objectives (i) and (ii), a desk research and literature review of the current knowledge of the three technologies was conducted. To add more current and specialized information, this phase has been supplemented with in-depth interviews with experts in the domain of those technologies.

Objective (iii) was reached by organizing eight focus groups, each consisting of 6–12 participants, in Belgian cities especially chosen according to the 'Dexia typology' to allow for as much diversity as possible.[3] With the help of prevention agencies and contacts within the police and the municipality, we managed to reach a total of 71 citizens willing to participate. Information and invitations were sent through social media and websites. Furthermore, letters were sent to citizens who had already gotten prevention advice from the prevention service. For each focus group we tried to find a balance between men and women to have all ages represented (under 25 and above 60 years old). The current study, however, does not aim at representing the opinion of Belgian citizens on the use of the new technologies in their private spaces. The goal of this project is exploratory and aims to analyse data within a defined group; to gather ideas, views and personal experiences surrounding these technologies; and to achieve a better view on diversity, as well as possibly opposite points of view. Qualitative interview records were transcribed and, together with field notes of unrecorded interviews and observations, analysed through repeated reading, coding and making annotations.

Focus-group discussions were based on cases and statements that allowed us to evaluate the citizens' perspective on the acceptability and self-sufficiency and expectations towards the (potential) use of three types of technology: home automation, biometrics and track and trace. A semi-structured, but flexible, discussion guide with questions was used. In the second part, to keep a broad focus and not to be limited by the imaginative capacity of citizens, two interactive focus groups with a total of seven experts and 13 in-depth interviews were organized to verify our results (Decorte, 2011). The experts were chosen by a purposive non-random sample, which means that the criteria of people interviewed is the most important thing in selecting them. The domain of theft prevention and new online security technologies were used as essential characteristics of the experts to be selected to reflect the diversity and breadth of the sample population. Next, an expert interviewed was asked if he or she could suggest other potential respondents, which is called 'snowball sampling' (Decorte, 2011). The focus groups provided an interesting interaction between expert views, while the interviews were useful to become familiar with the topic in a more 'practical way' or to get deeper into a certain subject. The interviews took an average of one hour; the focus groups, two hours.

These strategies ended up in an inventory of citizens' needs and questions as (potential) individual users of those three technologies, as well as current and efficient information to find a solution for the accompanied challenges. This information was collected in a manual to support the work of the theft prevention advisors when they give advice to citizens (objective (iv)). In this chapter, a short description of the theoretical concepts will be given. Afterwards, we focus on the citizen perceptions, but also on the view and knowledge of the experts, and conclude with some recommendations.

Crime-enhancing or crime-fighting technology in the case of domestic burglary

Criminal events, such as domestic burglary, vary in time and circumstances. New technologies that change the societal development are exploited by both criminals and crime fighters either to maximize and facilitate activities (crime-enhancing technology) or to do the opposite, i.e. minimizing or controlling them (crime-fighting technology) (Nuth, 2008). Crime conducted through the Internet – 'cybercrime', 'Internet-related crime', 'computer crime' – is no exception to this 'law'. What all these terminologies imply is that the advent of technology has a significant role in: (i) making crime possible, (ii) creating (new) criminal opportunities and (iii) committing traditional crime in a modern way (FTC, 2015).

Securing one's home, which has traditionally been accomplished by other means, for example by good door locks (i.e. 'construction-related measures') and not 'hiding a key under the doormat' (i.e. 'organizational measures') (Schoeters, 2012), can now be executed via the Internet, 'a computer-related venue' or some other technological computing advancement. This can, however, make property extra vulnerable to risks that are typical for the Internet, computer-related venues or other technological computing advancements (FTC, 2015).

The Internet intruding upon our 'Things'

For a long time now, developments in technology have been assisting efforts to tackle the challenges of crime (Nuth, 2008). It should be noted that the term 'new technologies' encompasses many aspects of information technology and is part of the broader concept of the 'Internet of Things' (hereafter the IoT). The IoT refers to everyday objects that have the ability to connect to the Internet, each other and the environment to produce, store, transmit and communicate information and data (FTC, 2015).

The number of Internet-connected devices surpassed the number of human beings on the planet in 2011 and experts estimate that by 2020, Internet-connected devices are expected to number between 26 billion and 50 billion (FTC, 2015; Skarþauskienë and Kalinauskas, 2015). This means the technology market is inevitably moving into the private sphere and homes of citizens.

The IoT will offer numerous and potentially revolutionary benefits to consumers, including, for example, distance detection or verification of intruders into one's home through surveillance cameras or energy efficiency support through smart meters (Jacobsson, Boldt and Carlsson, 2016).

As for risks, however, the IoT presents a variety of potential security threats that could be exploited to harm consumers by: (i) enabling unauthorized access and misuse of personal information; (ii) facilitating attacks on other systems; and (iii) creating risks to personal safety (FTC, 2015). In addition, technological innovations are likely to have both intended and unintended consequences for crime and social control: (i) potential negative effects on individual fundamental rights and freedom, including privacy; (ii) investing scarce resources in technology applications rather than in (more effective and) other measures of prevention and control; (iii) pressure to replace people (social informal control) by different forms of 'thing' technology; (iv) continued development and expansion of control strategies; and (v) consequences of activating the arms race between criminals and crime fighters (FTC, 2015).

Scenarios of the Internet of Things in the private homes of citizens

Home automation systems

A popular application of new technologies to avert burglary is to include different electronic connections, such as autonomously scheduling the lights or an Internet-connected radio or TV to simulate presence when the house is actually unoccupied. Consequently, this also offers remote control of different security systems within the home, for example: keeping an eye on (video) camera images, turning on the alarm when one has forgotten this while leaving the house or getting a (warning) message when the alarm has been activated. While this kind of technology appears to have clear advantages, using appliances in such a way can come with drawbacks: the home can become physically vulnerable to new threats in the form of intrusion attempts that are usually associated with traditional online interaction – they could get hacked (Jacobsson, Boldt and Carlsson, 2016).

The most common points of attack are users' passwords and Internet connections. Hackers could get inside a network, then inside the home, as they may be able to open a door, disarm an alarm or inspect on camera what is inside one's home. Digital logs of someone's patterns and habits, if left unsecured and targeted by hackers, could leave the inhabitants vulnerable too. This brings us to what is called 'the risk of concept drift' or 'function creep', which means that information is used for other intentions than the original purpose of collection

The influence of technological innovations 49

(Reuter, 2013; Jacobsson, Boldt and Carlsson, 2016). Digital traces, consciously or unconsciously left by users, and typically developed for other purposes, can be used to build extensive personal profiles of the residents of a home. As such, criminals can be gathering intelligence to know, for example, when you are about to leave and when you are coming home, which may in turn support the plan for how to best manifest a physical break-in (Ding *et al.*, 2014; Jacobsson, Boldt and Carlsson, 2016).

The threats posed to IoT-connected homes relate mainly to privacy disclosure, inadequate access control and malware mitigation. Related to the hardware of the devices, theft, manipulation and sabotage of the various devices and servers are additional risks. However, it is the end-users themselves that represent one of the weakest links, as the lack of or a poor selection of passwords is currently the biggest threat. Flawed passwords may lead to unauthorized redistribution of confidential information and to hacking exploitation attacks (Jacobsson *et al.*, 2016). A lack of authentication in this case means that anyone who figures out the IP address for a particular device, a camera for example, could watch the camera's stream and thus (mis)use the device.

Not only the end-users but also providers have responsibility in this case. Systems are often made crawlable by search engines (i.e. they show up in search results) and due to certain providers that do not require user names and passwords by default in a now-discontinued product, people (in the worst case: criminals) are able to click on the links, which gives them the ability to turn these people's homes into robbery targets. Opening a garage door, for example, could make a house conducive to actual physical intrusion (ENISA, 2015).

Biometrics

The previous part shows that one of the biggest problems for home (network) security is the authentication system. Most security systems mainly use and rely on passwords; standard passwords or simple passwords, making it easy for unauthorized users to intrude on the system. Access card authentication is another essential for many modern access control systems. Fighting breaches due to reasons such as loss, stolen or unauthorized duplications of the access cards is increasingly a challenge (Kindt and Dumortier, 2008).

Next to adequate password protection, biometrics technology is considered a better – or additional – protection method of user information, data, etc. Basically, biometrics technology will collect and measure data of human physiology or behavioural patterns, as its main purpose is to identify and verify a person's identity. There are several ways to collect and measure the data of users, such as scanning the unique characteristics of a person (i.e. finger-print, retina, facial expression) or analysing behaviour (i.e. signature, keyboard typing styles) (Wayne, 2002).

Biometrics technology is more convenient than other protection technologies of identity authentication as it is neither easily forgotten nor easily duplicated/copied (which could increase the risk of unauthorized physical access or access to important data) (Wayne, 2002). Although there are many advantages of

50 *Kim Van Hoorde* et al.

biometrics security systems, they are marked by several flaws. Particularly reference data, which are required from each user enrolled in an authentication system and which are used for comparison during subsequent authentication processes, need to be protected from malicious use (Vielhauer, 2006). Criminal activity depends on how resistant (i.e. 'hack-proof') biometric systems are to security threats and risks posed from outside third parties. Latent fingerprints, for example, can be left behind in a sensor and be used to produce what is known as a dummy print, which could possibly be used to fool a biometric system (i.e. 'spoofing'). This can be avoided, however, when a fingerprint biometric system is used, which requires that a live fingerprint be read – a system supported by temperature, electrical conductivity, and blood flow. This is important, as it greatly reduces the risk of spoofing. Another disadvantage of biometrics as a single scheme for user authentication is simply the fact that they are supposed to be unique and not replaceable. This means that once a specific biometric feature is compromised for a user, it cannot easily be replaced by another (Vielhauer, 2006). Moreover, the use of biometric templates that fall outside their intended use could result in the degradation of the sense of anonymity and cause privacy rights issues (Das, 2014).

Single-factor authentication usually consists of 'something you know'. Generally, however, these could be susceptible to attacks that could compromise the security of the application. Some of the more common attacks can occur at little or no cost to the perpetrator and without detection. Therefore, access control should ideally combine 'something you know' (i.e. a password), 'something you have' (i.e. a badge) and 'something you are' (i.e. a fingerprint) (Kindt and Dumortier, 2008).

Track and trace

When burglars have been successful, technology still creates a possibility to enable visibility and traceability of (stolen) products. One promising approach is Radio-Frequency-Identification ('RFID'). This means that each product is equipped with a unique (RFID) tag that can be read in a contactless fashion in order to track the movement of the product (Mangard and Schaumont, 2015).

A global positioning system (GPS) also makes it possible to identify a particular location with precision and minimal time, which might be beneficiary not only for the owners, but also for police work in cases of theft. Track-and-trace technology is very useful because it can facilitate intelligent assistance and recovery of the vehicle or mobile device (Nuth, 2008), which, with regard to domestic burglary, are the most familiar applications of track-and-trace systems.

The most significant risks of track-and-trace systems are related to location data and identity data. The data may be used in marketing purposes or for illegal surveillance (Skarþauskienë and Kalinauskas, 2015).

Social perception and citizens' acceptance of technology

Different studies have focused on the public assessment of Information Systems (IS) and the factors that may hamper or reinforce public acceptability of technology.

Several competing and complementary models, each with a different set of acceptance determinants, have been developed and evolved over the years.

Previous studies have considered citizens' acceptance under the premise that technology acceptance would bring prosperity and wealth. Other classic studies used a 'deficit model', arguing that the level or lack of scientific knowledge must be considered as an independent variable and the level of support for science and technology as the dependent variable (Pavone, Esposti and Santiago, 2013). New approaches emphasized the importance of socio-cultural factors, like trust, and the need to take into account lay knowledge as a relevant type of knowledge and the experience of citizens in the decisions process about the directions of science and technology to guarantee socially robust and publicly shared development of new technologies (Pavone *et al.*, 2013).

In 1985, Fred Davis suggested the Technology Acceptance Model (TAM). It examines the mediating role of perceived ease of use and perceived usefulness in their relation between system characteristics (external variables) and the probability of system use (an indicator of system success) (Davis, Bagozzi and Warshaw, 1989). More recently, extended versions of this model were suggested, which include social influence processes (subjective norm, voluntariness, and image) and cognitive instrumental processes (job relevance, output quality, result demonstrability, and perceived ease of use) (Venkatesh and Davis, 2000).

Like earlier acceptance and adoption models, the Unified Theory of Acceptance and Use of Technology (UTAUT) of Venkatesh *et al.* (2003) aims to explain user intentions to use an IS and further the usage behaviour. This synthesized model presents a more complete picture of the acceptance process than any previous individual model has been able to do by merging into one integrated model eight separate models previously used in the IS literature, all of which had their origins in psychology, sociology and communication. UTAUT holds that four key constructs (performance expectancy, effort expectancy, social influence and facilitating conditions) are direct determinants of usage intention and behaviour (Venkatesh *et al.*, 2003).

A more recent study, called the SurPRISE project (EU, KP7 program), aims at empirically investigating criteria and factors likely to affect public acceptance and acceptability of Surveillance Oriented Security Technology (SOSTs) in Europe. According to this research we should take into account familiarity with and general attitudes towards SOSTs, perceived intrusiveness and effectiveness, temporal, spatial and social proximity, as well as the perceived level of security threat, institutional trustworthiness and privacy concerns (Pavone *et al.*, 2013).

The objective of this study is to identify factors that influence public acceptance of and expectations towards new technologies. As mentioned before, the final target and the determinant factor of any innovation is the user who is able to operate and willing to pay for it. The rational arguments about life-facilitating features and the myriad opportunities of the IoT may not be heard by the end-user if he does not understand the potential and possible benefits of technology. On the other hand, rational proof about the risks of the IoT may not be considered by the end-user if he has no correct and full understanding of the

52 *Kim Van Hoorde* et al.

challenges of technology. The experience and engagement elements of users are the key components for the success of the IoT (Skarþauskienë and Kalinauskas, 2015). Based on the aforementioned acceptance models in the literature, we created our own determinants to give an overview and get a better understanding of users' acceptance and use of the selected new technologies, which will be described in the next part.

The citizen perspective and knowledge of experts

In this section, we introduce the results of the focus groups with both the citizens and experts and describe their perspectives on burglary and theft, as well as their view on security measures and privacy.

Perceptions of burglary and theft

The importance of the IoT in burglary and theft prevention has consequences for risk and victimization of burglary and theft. The thin line between the 'classical' risks of 'physical intrusion', on the one hand, and the 'new' risks of our 'virtual door', on the other, will fade away. There is no consensus on this matter, however, among experts who were interviewed. Some of them are very clear and try to warn citizens about the dangers of the Internet. They predict an increase of online crime involving the use of citizens' data and IoT objects. Other experts are more moderate and have the opinion that, for now, not citizens but companies are the most important victims of online crime and 'cyber theft'. Nowadays, most thefts and burglaries committed towards individuals are usually committed in the classical way, i.e. through physical intrusion. Experts believe that when perpetrators make an analysis of their costs and benefits, the more classic methods still offer higher gains than domestic burglary 'through cyber space', i.e. hacking into a connected house, which may enable opening electric doors or disarming the alarm, for example. Most professionals, however, conclude that when the IoT becomes more significant in use, cyber-attacks may increase.

This reality or prediction has an important implication. The limited knowledge of citizens about the opportunities and possible threats of the IoT, even widespread in the media, does not stimulate them to take actions to protect their electronic communication and systems against attacks. Citizens do recognize the potential problem, but underestimate the dangers. When they should protect themselves and take preventive measures, they do not feel the need to do so. 'You should trust people' or 'that is something I do not worry about at the moment; that is something for the future' were arguments reported by the participants (citizens).

Results show that citizens' expectations and attitudes are constructed by their own perceptions of the modus operandi of the perpetrators, but also by their own perception of the use and the value of the security systems. Citizens see a difference between professional and occasional criminals. The occasional thief will

The influence of technological innovations   53

operate from a 'rational choice' (Cornish and Clarke, 2008). This means that people involved in crime weigh the costs or consequences against the benefits. Situational crime prevention measures, in that case, gain importance. For most citizens, the rational choice is also a starting point to motivate their choice for target hardening.

Concerning the 'professional' offenders, citizens have a more fatalistic attitude. 'You cannot stop them', they often said. Other studies confirm that victims often have the opinion that they cannot prevent such organized crimes (Kerkab and Deroover, 2012).

Furthermore, citizens evaluate the risk of being a victim of burglary or theft as very low. People usually take action once it is already too late, and consequently become the victim of the criminal activity (Christiaensen and Dormaels, 2012). After a while, people also become less alert. Looking at online victimization (identity theft, hacking ...), people are even more careless. The feeling of being anonymous ('why should they pick me?') shows that people are less careful and make less safe decisions because they have the feeling of being in a secured environment. In this kind of situation a lot of warnings and suspicious signals are not registered or simply ignored.

Knowledge of electronic and technological systems

Know-how of and experience with technological security systems and the Internet is not that common for most of the citizen participants. They have the feeling that they do not have sufficient affinity with the security measures to know whether a system is effective or how to determine the quality of what they buy. This lack of know-how is undermining the confidence in 'new' technologies; however, even citizens who do have a good technological know-how do not always believe in the effectiveness of those systems.

Despite a clear scepticism, most citizens are aware of the technological (r)evolution of our society. They are convinced that citizens themselves should take responsibility for understanding these new trends. Currently, some people are not familiar with the use of technology, which may hinder them from trying out new technologies.

Burglary prevention: electronic security as a measure of preference?

With respect to preventive measures against burglary, in general, participants in our study prefer organizational measures, followed by construction-related measures. Electronic measures are the least preferred measures. As such, most citizens seem to follow the logic of techno-preventive advice ('OBER/OFEM principle'[4]). They wonder what benefit there is to 'a door with a good lock or an alarm system if the key is left underneath a flowerpot'. By this means, electronic systems were often perceived as 'expensive', 'unreliable' and 'easily misused'. In addition, some citizens use more 'ideological' arguments against technological measures and consider these systems as 'impersonal', 'asocial' or even 'repulsive'.

54   *Kim Van Hoorde* et al.

Some citizens, however, disagree with the majority by favouring electronic measures. Somewhat ironically, they consider these systems as 'more reliable' compared to 'error-prone humans'. They refer to the fact that humans 'monitor or observe only selectively' while 'technology monitors continuously' and consider it an additional advantage that, by using technology, 'you can verify the situation at home at all times'. Furthermore, they hint at a possible 'deterrence effect' when pictograms signal the presence of electronic security. They refer to the idea that 'time is a scarce resource for burglars and when in doubt, they will be inclined to choose a different target'.

Next to the discussion on the effectiveness of measures, there was much debate on whether to rely on 'informal forms of social control'. Some participants consider social cohesion in the neighbourhood and neighbours, who can keep an eye on suspicious activity, as an effective way to limit the chance of theft and burglary. Technology cannot replace the need for these forms of social control: 'if you receive a warning that an alarm system has been activated, it is important to have friendly neighbours willing to assess the situation'. However, most citizens agree that these forms of social control have their limitations. Not all people are willing to intervene in case of a suspicious situation or people may read a situation as less problematic than the reality requires. In addition, social control will be less effective during the daytime when many people are absent from home.

When evaluating the perceptions of citizens with respect to the role of technology, we should differentiate between individuals who see more value in the preventive effect and individuals who stress the possibilities technology offers with respect to reaction. Again, this difference relates to various ideas citizens have on the methods that criminals use and the individual's perception of the risks of becoming victimized.

Some citizens assume that burglars are 'lazy' and when they suspect the presence of electronic prevention measures, 'they will prefer to choose a new and (less protected) target'. Some citizens disagree, however; they warn that 'the presence of electronic protection may signal the presence of valuable goods'.

As a reactive measure, technology may be useful by sending notices of a security breach to one's smartphone, by storing CCTV-images of the incident or by signalling the location of stolen goods when track-and-trace systems are implemented. As such, technology may help to identify perpetrators or help to retrieve goods.

Citizens argue against 'overprotection' as well. An idea often mentioned is that if perpetrators really want to burgle a house, they will eventually succeed. If the house is strongly protected, they may use more intrusive methods, increasing the risk of vandalism and destruction of property. They conclude that technology is a barrier that may in such cases delay burglary but not necessarily prevent it from happening.

Experts disagree on whether the IoT is currently already 'a door' that gives criminals access to a house. This lack of consensus may be explained by the difference in perspective related to the professional backgrounds of these experts. Experts with a background in security of businesses and companies are generally estimating the risk higher than experts specialized in securing private homes.

Differences also exist based on the way one sees technology as preventive or as a reactive measure. Some experts believe that petty thieves and burglars cannot be compared with hackers based on knowledge and skills. They consider the risks of burglary by means of abusing electronic systems currently as negligible. Blackmailing and extortion rather than burglary and theft are considered motives to break into networks in search of sensitive or compromising data.

According to the experts, however, more consensus exists regarding the trends for the near future. Two evolutions have been noted: (i) electronic security systems will increasingly become a target of attacks and (ii) a shift is occurring from attempts at burglary from the ground floor to the first floor of buildings (as few protective measure, construction-related or electronic, are on this level of buildings). Depending on the scale of implementation of specific technologies, a shift in focus may occur in methods used by criminals. An arms race exists between criminals and law enforcement agencies (or developers of security-related technologies) (Nuth, 2008) that results in a diminishing value of technology once criminals have adapted to its presence.

Experts emphasize that advice on theft/burglary prevention starts with the idea that priority should be given to the organizational and construction-related measures and that electronic measures are only a third line of defence. Nevertheless, the 'OBER/OFEM' principle with 'registration' and 'report'[5] remains important too: registration allows law enforcement agencies to identify the owner of stolen goods more easily. Owners of stolen goods can prove more quickly that these goods belong to them. This equally applies for online data that can be secured by storing them on an external hard-disk. Before law enforcement agencies are able to do this, however, the owner or witness should report the burglary or theft (Schoeters, 2012).

Perceptions on responsibility for security and prevention

The attribution of responsibility to protect the citizen's perspective is not a black-and-white story according to the citizens.

On the one hand, citizens argue that government authorities have the responsibility to protect the citizens: they see the relationship between civilians and government as a form of 'social contract' (Pavone, Esposti and Santiago, 2013). Some citizens argue that it is the responsibility of law enforcement agencies to be up to date with current evolutions with respect to ICT, at least if they want to avoid citizens taking the law in their own hands and if they want to protect the monopoly on the use of force. They recognize that law enforcement agencies often lack time and resources to localize and retrieve a smartphone following track-and-trace systems. However, they argue that the content of a smartphone may have great emotional value for people and they expect that police agents will not simply ignore the case.

56 *Kim Van Hoorde* et al.

Citizens, on the other hand, generally do not favour 'pampering' by government or strict government-induced obligations or prohibitions. As such, in some cases they are inclined to see the end-user of technology as somewhat responsible when he/she is victimized ('blaming the victim') and had not taken any precautionary measures. Nevertheless, they recognize that legally, only the thief can be held responsible, as he/she is the one breaking the law.

Experts suggest that end-users should carefully consider what systems or products they want to connect to the Internet. They argue that manufacturers, installers, ICT and software suppliers and other parties involved should build in security at the start of the development process ('security and privacy by design'). They should provide end-users with product information in such a way that it empowers them to take preventive measures. However, convincing the important players to take a more integrated approach towards the possibilities and pitfalls of technology with respect to theft/burglary is not an easy task. Manufacturers and suppliers want to address the needs and desires of potential clients even if this leads to security flaws. Architects, for example, are notoriously hard to involve in the process. Architectural training on building design as a means of prevention is limited and most architects as such do not fully recognize the importance of their role. Most experts, for example, favour sleek facades and windows that do not open whereas most architects consider these as unwanted limitations on their architectural freedom.

Government authorities have, according to citizens and experts, a key position because they can formulate and enforce standards for manufacturers and suppliers and monitor the market. In addition, government actors, in close cooperation with other partners, have an awareness-increasing role.

Concerns for privacy breaches

Because of further digitalization and integration of sensors and chips in the most diverse objects, data on users and objects will increase exponentially. Smart objects are already capable of analysing and recognizing characteristics of the environment and habits or preferences of individual users and act upon these aspects in an adequate way.

This results in increasing possibilities for criminals as well as governments and companies to gather information on behaviour, movements and preferences of citizens as individuals. The implications of these growing connections lead to fundamental questions and debate on citizens' privacy, confidentiality of data and potential new forms of crime. It remains to be seen whether criminals will hack CCTV systems to explore and select potential targets and study the ideal moments for burglary. Citizens wonder whether 'criminals will use track-and-trace systems to know where individuals are located and/or if they will target biometric data as a means towards identity theft'.

Although most citizens as respondents value privacy, few know what kind of privacy the law protects and does not protect. What guides citizens' attitudes is not so much the definition that the legal frameworks offer, but their personal

The influence of technological innovations   57

sense of what privacy looks like and their perception of when it is violated. Views on privacy are as such primarily emotion-based and open to change depending on the arguments that come up during the focus group discussions. Citizens appear particularly critical when it comes to companies that sell users' data for profit.

Citizens acknowledge that in order to use technology or download apps, they 'have to give up' some privacy, but they do not experience this as a 'real choice': 'informed consent' declarations for users are not really informative, as they are written in legal jargon and they obscure the real consequences of acceptance. Moreover, professionals warn that privacy often colludes with the 'ease of use', the latter often being a priority for users. Privacy-protecting measures may complicate the ease of use and it remains an open question to what degree users are willing to trade one for the other.

Application restrictions of a new technology concerning the prevention of burglary

Although technology holds a number of clear promises in order to provide a complete and integrated approach to the prevention of burglary, the expectations may not be at odds. After all, various problems crop up.

According to the theft prevention advisors and experts questioned, the first problem refers to the fact that it is difficult to sell investments in high-tech security devices (and protection in general). The results of precautionary measures are not immediately perceptible. One cannot know whether the attempt to break in was prevented because of those measurements taken. It concerns the more advanced technological systems in particular, because citizens are convinced that these are expensive.

Another restriction is the fact that technology is sometimes too 'isolated'; this means that the integration of these objects in daily life indeed occurs, but the factual daily usage remains rather limited. This points to a gradual change in the position and the way people behave, but also stresses the fact that consumers are not always waiting for all the possibilities of technology. The applications are, for example, too 'technology-driven': the focus was especially on the technical possibilities but the social desirability was not sufficiently taken into account. When there is too little reflection about the user-friendliness of the systems, it is not unthinkable that many citizens will pull out.

In general, the phenomenon of the 'arms race' points out that, although new technology creates new opportunities concerning security, burglars can rapidly adapt their method of working whether or not they are using the same technology. Something may be well secured today, but can be totally superseded tomorrow. Criminals (and ethical hackers) are constantly looking for weak points in security, both physical and online security. For certain citizens this is hard to accept. They do not grasp where it ends, and if they perceive that they have already missed the (technology-) train, they pull out completely due to the fast developments within this domain. They are 'not fully acquainted', 'it is too

Discussion

The recent confluence of key technologies and market trends is ushering in a new reality for the 'Internet of Things'. The question is, will the prospect of the IoT as a ubiquitous array of devices bound to the Internet fundamentally change how people think about what it means to be 'online'? Therefore, this research project wanted to study (i) the potential of a fully interconnected 'smart' world, with objects and people, as well as objects and their environment, becoming more tightly intertwined, and (ii) how users experience technology as such. Do they accept the terms that come along with smart devices and do citizens possess the accurate and required knowledge to not let these security measures become an additional threat to their physical and online 'possessions'?

Before the results and the recommendations linked to this topic are discussed in more detail, it is advisable to dwell upon the often only 'superficial' knowledge that is present among citizens with respect to the IoT, and the specific application as home electronics, biometrics and track and trace. These data are the leitmotiv through the research.

Technological developments related to the IoT happen in rapid succession. Product developers and providers lose no time in introducing new devices. Nevertheless, many innovations in the sphere were yet not discovered by the users and few citizens have experience with (the advanced systems of) home electronics, biometrics and track and trace. Consequently, it seems that citizens consider the IoT and their connected possibilities and threats as far removed from their personal lives, rather than a reality that announces itself today and tomorrow.

After all, we seem to be on the eve of a revolution. Apple recently announced it was installing the Apple HomeKit in order to make it easier for smart accessories to communicate, and for the user to connect and manage all the smart accessories in his home from various manufacturers. The citizen is slightly aware of the development itself, but in no way gives a moment of thought to the dangers that may be linked to it. The knowledge of the citizen lags behind with regard to usage and the dangers of those means and especially the dangers they may involve.

The question arises regarding to what extent citizens run the risk of becoming a victim of the safety risks that are linked to the IoT. Some experts indicate that the chances of being victimized are still real. Others consider this as something of the (near) future. At this moment, considered from a cost/benefit perspective, the more classical burglary techniques are probably still the most efficient, therefore it is still only marginally beneficial to burglars to apply 'cyber activities' to obtain their loot. Most of the experts, however, agree that as the IoT has more and more applications and will be implemented on a larger scale by citizens, this can/will change rapidly.

The influence of technological innovations 59

This finding has a number of important implications. The lack of knowledge and experience of the citizens about the chances and threats of the IoT, fed by the stories 'from the media' (and to a more limited degree through the victims of their network), does not help them take adequate actions: implementing electronic security and properly securing the electronic systems.

Given the pace at which technology evolves, the lack of practical experience with the IoT and the rather superficial knowledge that dominates this subject among a lot of citizens, it would not be wise for the government to wait until the IoT becomes really relevant with regard to burglary and theft. The government has to act now, proactively and preventively, and has to study up for challenges that will present themselves in the short and long term. The insight concerning the way one thinks about and approaches these phenomena is important to adapt the composition. The insecurity and questions that arise at the moment have to be a point of departure for a policy; besides the implementation of a number of general recommendations (see infra), sound information distribution and an active awareness-raising in particular need to be high on the agenda.

Recommendations

As the implementation of the IoT expands, the risks that go hand in hand with it also grow. It is possible that the modus operandi of the burglary and theft perpetrators will shift. Nowadays, citizens are not very aware of the problems and dispose of little knowledge to follow and estimate the rapid changes. A proactive policy is desirable, and it is not recommendable to start from a blank page: a lot of principles and frameworks developed as part of classic burglary and theft prevention remain extremely important, but ought to be translated into the IoT framework. The citizen should change his way of thinking, as well as his awareness, that houses not only have a front door, but that more and more of those houses also have an electronic entrance. Information and awareness raising are the best tools to help realize that change.

One key approach would be to create an adequate *environmental design*, for which it is best to start up a 'traditional partners' network of insurance companies, clients, police, architects and theft prevention advisors. It is also, however, advisable to seek the advice of manufacturers, (software) developers and IT-specialists, fitters (private security) and technical universities within the scope of the 'new technology'.

An integral approach further demands a breakthrough of the insular culture between various agents engaged with those problems (police, theft prevention advisors, professional federations ...). Cooperation between the public and private sector may lead to surplus value in the process of integrating already existing technologies. An ideal scenario in the future: (1) definition of the needs; (2) consideration of what is developing; and (3) mutual harmony. Every citizen should be approached with an equal harmony. An important question, however, is 'who is "the citizen"?' Is everyone capable of using those applications? And what about the high-risk groups? Depending on the needs and the capital, and the capacities and time that one can/may invest, the choice and usage of certain technologies will differ.

Two recommendations occupy centre stage with regard to the supply of information: establish a centre of knowledge that centralizes and spreads information to professional agents, and to develop local anchors where the citizens can get help or advice. Within this scope, one indicates the value for citizens of an 'approachable' helpdesk (linked to and nourished by the 'centre of knowledge') that provides answers to all possible questions concerning technology and security. This helpdesk can be situated on different levels (level of ministry or the local police or on another level). The question of which channel is best to use to help citizens (local or federal) may help us to rethink the role of the theft prevention advisors.

On a last note, we strongly recommend prioritizing the alerting of the problems of unsecured wireless networks (those fully accessible on the Internet because the user does not provide them with a simple password). This is a relatively simple aspect that, when acted upon, produces a number of *quick gains*. Just like the other campaigns involving the phenomena that demand uninterrupted vigilance of the citizen (BOB-campaign: designated driver), campaigns should preferably be continuously and systematically repeated. Moreover, the campaign should be 'empowering' and aim at the specific safety problems, for example providing information on how one can secure a specific home electronics device in a number of steps, rather than information on the general security aspects.

Notes

1 The philosophy of domestic burglary prevention makes a distinction between three types of security measures (Schoeters, 2012): (i) organizational measures, as security starts with adopting good habits, are cheap and simple to carry out, such as efficient key control, increasing the visibility of the habitation and concealing valuable objects; (ii) construction-related measures or strengthening and securing the façade elements, by placing, for example, shatterproof glass or a security cylinder, which make up an extra obstacle for burglars; and (iii) electronic measures or placing alarm and detection systems as a completion of the other measures. It is important to adopt the measures in this order to guarantee an optimal security. Executing mechanical or electronic measures would not be of much use if organizational measures are not observed. This means that installing a good alarm makes no sense if citizens leave their door unlocked. Organizational measures therefore form the foundation for successful security against domestic burglary.
2 Commissioned by the Directorate Local Integral Security of the Belgian Federal Government Service of Internal Affairs.
3 The so-called Dexia typology of municipalities allows for a division of the 589 fused municipalities in Belgium into 'only' six categories (based on 11 factors), as opposed to other less pragmatic typologies that often make use of a division containing over 10 categories. We selected at least one city out of each category.
4 See supra.
5 The 'OBER/OFEM' principle stands for organizational, construction-related, electronic measures and registration/report, which are all important to consider in order to obtain optimal prevention/security.

References

Byrne, J. and Marx, G., 2011–2013. Technological innovations in crime prevention and policing: a review of the research on implementation and impact. *Cahiers Politiestudies*, 20, pp. 17–40.

Christiaensen, S. and Dormaels, A., 2012. De neuzen in dezelfde, juiste richting: de beheersing van diefstal in woningen vanuit integraal en geïntegreerd perspectief. In: S. Christiaensen, A. Dormaels and S. Van Daele, eds., *Diefstal in woningen. Bijdragen voor een geïntegreerde beheersing vanuit beleid, praktijk en wetenschap.* Antwerpen-Apeldoorn: Maklu.

Corbett, R. and Marx, G., 1991. Critique: no soul in the new machine: technofallacies in the electronic monitoring movement. *Justice Quarterly*, 8(3), pp. 359–414.

Cornish, D.B. and Clarke, R., 2008. *The rational choice perspective: environmental criminology and crime analysis.* Portland, OR: Willan Publishing.

Das, R., 2014. *Biometric technology: authentication, biocryptography, and cloud-based architecture.* New York: CRC Press.

Davis, F.D., Bagozzi, R.P. and Warshaw, P.R., 1989. User acceptance of computer technology: a comparison of two theoretical models. *Management Science*, 35(8), pp. 982–1003.

Decorte, T., 2011. *Methoden van onderzoek: ontwerp en dataverzameling. Een handleiding.* Gent: Academia Press.

Ding, A.Y., Hafeez, I., Tarkoma, S., Krischenko, A. and Stalberg, M., 2014. *Securing smart homes: opportunities, risks, and techniques* [pdf]. University of Helsinki and F-Secure Corporation. Available at: http://docplayer.net/7021098-Smart-homes-bring-many-comforting-and-time-saving.html [accessed on February 12, 2015].

Ekblom, P., 2005. Designing products against crime. In: N. Tilley, ed., *Handbook of crime prevention and community safety.* Cullompton, UK: Willan Publishing. pp. 203–244.

ENISA, 2015. *Threat landscape and good practice guide for smart home and converged media* [online]. Available at: www.enisa.europa.eu/activities/risk-management/evolving-threat-environment/enisa-thematic-landscapes/threat-landscape-for-smart-home-and-media-convergence [accessed on June 16, 2015].

FTC, 2015. *Internet of things: privacy and security in a connected world* [pdf]. Federal Trade Commission. Available at: www.ftc.gov/system/files/documents/reports/federal-trade-commission-staff-report-november-2013-workshop-entitled-internet-things-privacy/150127iotrpt.pdf [accessed on April 24, 2015].

Jacobsson, A., Boldt, M. and Carlsson, B., 2016. A risk analysis of a smart home automation system. *Future Generation Computer Systems*, 56, pp. 719–733.

Kerkab, R. and Deroover, M., 2012. Naburig herhaald slachtofferschap bij woninginbraken: een verkenning van nieuwe paden voor het inbraakpreventiebeleid. In: S. Christiaensen, A. Dormaels and S. Van Daele, eds., *Diefstal in woningen. Bijdragen voor een geïntegreerde beheersing vanuit beleid, praktijk en wetenschap.* Antwerpen: Maklu, pp. 47–70.

Kindt, E. and Dumortier, J., 2008. Biometrie als herkenning- of identificatiemiddel? Enkele juridische beschouwingen. *Computerrecht: Tijdschrift voor Informatica, Telecommunicatie en Recht*, 132, pp. 185–198.

Mangard, S. and Schaumont, P., 2015. *Radio frequency identification: security and privacy issues.* New York: Springer.

Nuth, M.S., 2008. Taking advantage of new technologies: for and against crime. *Computer Law & Security Report*, 24, pp. 437–446.

62 *Kim Van Hoorde* et al.

Pavone, V., Esposti, S.D. and Santiago, E., 2013. *Surveillance, privacy and security: a large scale participatory assessment of criteria and factors determining acceptability and acceptance of security technologies in Europe* [pdf]. Seventh Framework Program. Available at: http://surprise-project.eu/wp-content/uploads/2013/10/SurPRISE-D2.2-Draft-Report-on-Key-Factors.pdf [accessed on February 18, 2015].

Reuter, T., 2013. *Security analysis of wireless communication standards for home automation*. Master's thesis in informatics. Universität München, Fakultät für Informatik.

Rose, K., Eldridge, S. and Chapin, L., 2015. *The internet of things: an overview. Understanding the issues and challenges of a more connected world* [pdf]. Internet Society. Available at: www.internetsociety.org/sites/default/files/ISOC-IoT-Overview-20151014_0.pdf [accessed on January 15, 2015].

Schoeters, I., 2012. Een rationele technopreventie: anticiperen op het inbraakproces. In: S. Christiaensen, A. Dormaels and S. Van Daele, eds., Diefstal in woningen. Bijdragen voor een geïntegreerde beheersing vanuit beleid, praktijk en wetenschap. Antwerpen: Maklu, pp. 135–152.

Skarþauskienė, A. and Kalinauskas, M., 2015. The internet of things: when reality meets expectations. *International Journal of Innovation and Learning*, 17(2), pp. 262–274.

Venkatesh, V. and Davis, F.D., 2000. A theoretical extension of the technology acceptance model: four longitudinal field studies. *Management Science*, 46, pp. 186–204.

Venkatesh, V., Morris, M.G., Davis, G.B. and Davis, F.D., 2003. User acceptance of information technology: toward a unified view. *Management Information Systems Quarterly*, 27(3), pp. 425–478.

Vielhauer, C., 2006. *Biometric user authentication for IT security: from fundamentals to handwriting*. Advances in information security. Dordrecht: Springer.

Wayne, P., 2002. *Biometrics: a double edged sword – security and privacy* [online]. SANS Institute. Available at: www.sans.org/reading-room/whitepapers/authentication/biometrics-double-edged-sword-security-privacy-137 [accessed on May 7, 2015].

4 When it rains in Paris, it drizzles in Brussels?

Hans Vermeersch, Ellen Vandenbogaerde and Evelien De Pauw

Introduction

For almost two decades, terror attacks in the global North (9/11, Madrid 2004, London 2005, Paris 2015 and Brussels 2016) have raised debate and concerns about appropriate anti-terrorism measures that could affect civil liberties, including the right to privacy (Haubrich, 2003; Posner, 2008; Dragu, 2011). As a result of the unpredictability and global repercussions of criminal actions, particularly those related to terror, a safer society is often pursued through the implementation of security policies that increasingly rely on the deployment of 'Surveillance-Orientated Security Technologies' (SOSTs) and interconnected data exchange systems.

These new technologies are often seen as fundamental elements in the management of increasingly unpredictable security risks. Nevertheless, they are often implemented based on the hope that 'they will be effective because they appear effective', in the absence of evidence-based research or without a careful analysis of potential and unintended consequences (Corbett and Marx, 1991; Byrne and Marx, 2011). It has often been assumed, moreover, that 'citizens value security more than privacy', referring to the 'if you have done nothing wrong, you have nothing to hide' attitude that is common in public opinion, and are thus more likely to accept this type of measure on the premise that more government control through surveillance increases their security (Solove, 2011). The debate about the use of SOSTs is often framed as a trade-off between privacy and security concerns, although this is only one among several potential interpretative frames by which the use of SOSTs can be evaluated (Pavone, Degli Esposti and Santiago, 2015). Results of the Surveillance Privacy and Security project (SURPRISE), a collaborative, mixed-methods research exercise to understand the views of residents of nine European countries on SOSTs, lead us to question the presumption that more security should necessarily go hand in hand with increasing intrusions of privacy. In fact, citizens want both effective security *and* protection of their privacy (see also Friedewald *et al.*, 2014). Furthermore, a lack of legal safeguards and transparency on the management of SOSTs undermines the perceived effectiveness of these technologies in the security domain (Degli Esposti and Gómez, 2015).

64 *Hans Vermeersch* et al.

In all, socio-demographic, cultural and attitudinal differences with respect to the acceptance of new technologies have been studied extensively over the past few years and several factors, e.g. trust in authorities managing these technologies, technology optimism, the perception of risks and threats, demographic attributes and socio-political attitudes, have been identified as contributing factors (Pavone and Degli Esposti, 2010; Smith, Dinev and Xu, 2011; Patil, 2015; Straus, 2015). It has been suggested that, in addition to these factors, 'external shocks or threats' like the aforementioned terror attacks could alter citizens' attitudes with respect to civil liberties and the acceptance of SOSTs (Huddy *et al.*, 2005). However, because such events are unpredictable by nature, it is difficult to study their impact, and studies often use experimental designs to simulate the effects of external shocks.

In this study, we evaluate the effects of real-world external shocks in the form of terror attacks that occurred in 2015, by using 2014 and 2016 panel data to analyse (i) whether respondents are more willing to trade privacy for government control, and (ii) whether this translates into higher acceptance of four specific technologies that can be used in the fight against crime in the general sense (and are often proposed measures in the fight against terrorism); smart CCTV, behavioural profiling, radio frequency identification (RFID) and DNA-databases.

The Paris attacks as a context for change in attitudes towards SOSTs?

Most studies on the potential impact of external shocks or threats use an experimental design. Lerner *et al.* (2003), for example, conducted an experiment where they randomly assigned participants to different texts and questions intended to induce fear, anger or sadness, and report that assignment to fear is associated with more conservative policy preferences (see also Huddy *et al.*, 2005). It is widely recognized that while fully randomized experimental designs allow for causal inferences, this comes at the cost of a lower external validity of results. Fully controlled experiments are artificial, and results can therefore not easily be generalized to the real world.

However, sometimes real-world events generate the conditions that allow for quasi-experimental designs. A limited number of studies combine real-world data with a research design suitable for causal inference. Research conducted in Spain at the time of the terror attack in Madrid, for example, provides evidence not only of a general shift towards more conservative political views as a consequence of the attack, but also an increase in anti-Arab sentiments (Echebarria-Echabe and Fernández-Guede, 2006). In addition, Bozzoli and Müller (2011) report a large and persistent effect of the London bombings on concerns about a future terror attack and a decreased support for civil liberties after the attack. Few studies, however, have measured the impact of terrorist events on the willingness to support the use of SOSTs and/or the variables that predict the use of SOSTs.

With respect to terror and the threat of terror, the year 2015 is often described as an 'annus horribilis' for Europe. Terror attacks in Paris reshaped public discourse on surveillance and privacy: the year started with attacks on the offices of satirical magazine Charlie Hebdo and a Jewish supermarket, was followed by increasingly callous attacks on random targets, such as shooting of tourists on a beach in Tunisia, and ended, again in Paris, with the deadliest attack since the Madrid bombings in 2004, the indiscriminate shooting of diners and concertgoers. The use of assault rifles to shoot inconspicuous targets at close range was a 'new' phenomenon in Europe that arguably changed the way citizen security is conceived, administered and managed. According to various commentators, the last attack in Paris in particular has, in its randomness and perceived uncontrollability, 'changed the face of the world', brought 'war to the West' and 'transformed our world for ever'.

The impact of the Paris attacks also strongly affected public discourse in Belgium: the risk of terror attacks climbed high on the agenda of both government and public opinion. The OCAD (Belgian Commission in charge of decisions concerning terror treatment and measures) decided to raise the terror threat level to the highest level, the Belgian army was on patrol, there was a house-to-house search in many streets, and the discussion of the police reform in Brussels and the pluralization of the police function by increasing the private security sector became hot topics on the policy agenda (Ponsaers, Devroe and Meert, 2006). The interconnectivity of France and Belgium's capital cities is reflected in the popular saying that is also the title of this contribution, 'when it rains in Paris, it drizzles in Brussels', suggesting that events and policy in Paris often diffuse to Brussels soon after. The fact that the attacks were at least partially planned and organized in Belgium and several suspects had Belgian nationality only increased this sentiment. The consensus in public discourse grew that it was only a matter of time before Belgium would be a target, sadly substantiated by coordinated terror attacks on Brussels soon after, in March 2016. It could be hypothesized that this change in public discourse and/or the salience of the threat and the concerns and anxieties it generated may substantially alter the 'privacy–control trade-off' and increase the support for the use of SOSTs.

This context roused interest in a battery of questions on the use of SOSTs by public authorities that were added to the 2014 wave of a panel study originally intended to evaluate attitudes of undergraduate students with respect to social and educational issues. More specifically, in 2014, we studied whether (i) framing SOSTs (smart CCTV, behavioural profiling, RFID, DNA-databases) either as a potential weapon against crime or as a threat to privacy influences student opinions, and (ii) whether that influence is moderated by pre-existing attitudes (privacy concerns, trust in public authorities, risk perception, technology optimism) of respondents. We found that framing effects in themselves were small, but that frames tend to interact with trust, privacy concerns and risk-perception. That is, rather than influence respondents to adopt a certain stance towards SOSTs, framing reinforced pre-existing attitudes (Vermeersch and De Pauw, 2017). These data allow for a follow-up study on the same study

66 *Hans Vermeersch* et al.

population, assessing whether the attacks in Paris have changed opinions on the use of SOSTs.

While other studies that have used real-world data to evaluate the effect of 'external shocks' on citizens' attitudes rely on comparisons of groups of respondents collected before and after the 'external shock', we were able to study the research questions based on two separate types of comparisons: group comparisons (comparing populations that uniquely participated in the 2014 or 2016 wave) as well as individual comparisons (a group of respondents that participated in both waves).

Research questions

Given the fact that our previous study on the acceptance of SOSTs dates from before the 2015 events, we decided that the same battery of questions should be repeated in the 2016 wave of our panel study in order to allow us to answer a set of questions about whether and how the Paris attacks may have influenced the opinions of the participants of our 2014 study.

Question 1: have the attacks in Paris changed students' opinions on trust in authorities, risk-perception, fear of crime, the attitudes on the 'privacy–control trade-off' and the use of SOSTs?

The literature discussed above suggests that external shocks may heighten perceived threats and anxiety and increase demand for government-provided security measures that could affect civil liberties, such as SOSTs. As mentioned before, a limited number of studies exist that combine real-world data with a research design suitable for causal inference (Echebarria-Echabe and Fernández-Guede, 2006; Bozzoli and Müller, 2011), yet few studies have looked at the effects of external shocks on the acceptance of SOSTs in particular. Moreover, most of these studies base their conclusions on a comparison of individuals who completed questionnaires before and after the external shocks. They were thus not able to address the change in individuals as a response to these shocks. As our study design was intended as a panel study, our data allow us to evaluate to what extent individual opinions have changed.

Furthermore, our data allow for evaluating two related questions. In 2016, we were specifically interested in the effects of a year of terrorism, so we added an additional experimental condition through randomly assigning respondents to terror and control frames. The terror frame showed graphic images of the 2015 attacks, increasing the immediate saliency thereof, and may thus have additional effects on the acceptance of SOSTs. In addition, the final phase of data collection coincided with the arrest of Paris' suspect Salah Abdeslam and subsequent coordinated attacks in Brussels. Although the number of respondents that answered the questionnaire after these events is relatively low, we can tentatively explore any additional effects of these events.

Question 2: is the change in opinions dependent on anxiety as a personality-variable?

It has been argued that terror attacks may influence attitudes regarding security and/or the use of SOSTs by public authorities through increasing the perception of an imminent threat to one's security. This would lead to more demand for government-provided security as individuals attempt to reduce discomfort, resulting from increased risk perceptions or increased fear (Davis and Silver, 2004). While little research has evaluated how terror attacks may have an impact on attitudes depending on personality factors, the fact that fear may be one of the factors that contributes to change in opinions as a result of the external shock may suggest that individuals who are anxiety prone may react more strongly to such an external shock. They may experience more discomfort and seek increased government-provided security as a result of the event, resulting in an increased acceptance of SOSTs and support for government control. Huddy *et al.* (2005) found that whilst heightened threat perceptions in the US increased support for surveillance policies, heightened anxiety did not have the same effects. They hypothesize that, because more anxious respondents are more risk averse, they are less likely to support policies that may involve additional risks and induce further anxiety. It may therefore be important to compare the change in attitudes between individuals who have a more anxious compared to a more emotionally stable personality.

Study design and sample characteristics

Sample

The research population for this study consists of undergraduate students of VIVES University College (Department of Applied Social Studies) located in Kortrijk, a medium-sized city in Southwest Flanders (Belgium).

Data were collected at two points: October–November 2014 and March–April 2016. All students registered at the Department were sent a survey invitation via the school's digital notice board and also received this invitation in their personal inboxes. Students were free to participate: participation was not required for and/or linked to any of the classroom activities. No incentives were offered for participation. The survey invitation included guarantees with respect to anonymity and data protection. Students could only participate by inserting a valid student registration code that could be used as a 'key-variable' for follow-up waves.

Four hundred and twenty students completed an online questionnaire in October–November 2014, and 299 completed the questionnaire in February–March 2016 (26% and 17% response rates, respectively[1]). This design allows for two independent comparisons:

- 113 students completed questionnaires in 2014 *and* in 2016, and their change in attitudes can be assessed by a repeated measures design (Group A).

68   *Hans Vermeersch* et al.

- In addition, 493 students completed the questionnaire in Wave 2014 (307) *or* in 2016 (186), allowing for comparisons between Wave 2014 and Wave 2016 (Group B).

The second wave of data collection coincided with the arrest of Paris' terror suspect Salah Abdeslam on March 18 and subsequent coordinated bomb attacks on the Brussels airport and a metro station on March 22. In 2016, 223 students completed the questionnaire before the arrest of Abdeslam, 61 thereafter and a further 15 after the Brussels attacks. We can thus also compare students who completed the 2016 questionnaire before and after these events.

Overall, this sample is of course not a random sample of the Belgian population and as such does not necessarily reflect general public attitudes; however, it is suitable to explore the effects of terror events on the opinions of this particular population.

Questionnaire and measurements

As was the case in 2014, we randomly assigned students to four different frames introducing SOSTs; a 'security' frame that introduced these technologies and highlighted their usefulness in the fight against crime, a 'privacy' frame that framed them in terms of potential infringements of privacy, a 'neutral' frame that included both 'security' and 'privacy' backgrounds, and a 'control' frame that introduced these technologies without further framing. Since our interest in 2016 was specifically related to terrorism, we also randomly[2] assigned respondents to two additional conditions; 'terrorism' and 'control' frames. The first showed respondents graphic images of attacks that occurred in 2015 and asked them about their emotional responses to terrorism, avoidance behaviour and perceptions of geographical as well as personal likelihood of becoming a victim of terrorism.[3]

In both waves, *Total acceptability of use of SOSTs* was measured by the sum of 'acceptability scores' of four types of technologies (RFID, DNA-data files, smart CCTV and behavioural profiling). Respondents received a vignette in which the technology was explained (see Appendix). Acceptability for each form was measured as the answer on a scale from 1 ('not acceptable at all') to 7 ('totally acceptable') on the question: 'In your opinion, is it acceptable that public authorities use this technology?' Cronbach's Alpha for this scale was 0.72 in 2014.

Privacy–control trade-off was measured by five items reflecting a willingness to trade privacy for security through government control (e.g. 'the government has too much power to track what we do in life') on a scale from 1 ('completely disagree') to 5 ('completely agree'), with higher scores indicating an inclination towards favouring more control for the government as opposed to privacy concerns. The sum of item scores was used. Cronbach's Alpha for this scale was 0.78 in 2014.

Trust in public authorities was measured on a scale from 1 ('do not trust at all') to 9 ('trust completely') by six items that measured trust in public authority instances (federal government, regional government, local government, police, judicial system, intelligence services). The sum of item scores was used. Cronbach's Alpha for this scale was 0.86 in 2014.

In both 2014 and 2016 we evaluated respondents' *personal assessments of safety* that, following Rountree and Land's (1996) conceptual distinction, can be divided into two components: cognitive (risk perception) and emotion-behavioural (fear of crime).

Risk perception was measured by five items indicating the risk a respondent perceives of being victimized by different forms of crime (aggression, theft, vandalism ...), on a scale from 1 ('no risk at all') to 5 ('very high risk'). The sum of item scores was used. Cronbach's Alpha for this scale was 0.72 in 2014.

Fear of crime was measured on a scale from 1 ('never') to 5 ('always') by four items including one emotional ('How safe do you feel in your neighbourhood?') and three behavioural items reflecting the occurrence of avoidance behaviours (avoiding certain areas, going out in darkness and answering the door to strangers). The sum of item scores was used. Cronbach's Alpha for this scale was 0.82 in 2014.

As mentioned, in 2016 we also included a personal assessment of *terror-related perceptions of safety* for half of the population (on a randomized base) including cognitive (risk perception) and emotion-behavioural components (fear of terrorism).

Terror-related risk perception was measured by four items indicating the perceived risk of a terror attack in Europe, Belgium and Kortrijk, and the risk of being personally affected by a terror attack, on a scale from 1 ('no risk at all') to 5 ('very high risk'). The sum of item scores was used. Cronbach's Alpha for this scale was 0.79.

Fear of terrorism was measured on a scale of 1 ('completely disagree') to 5 ('completely agree') by four items including one emotional 'I now feel less safe at big events and public places where many people convene' and three behavioural items reflecting the occurrence of avoidance behaviours (e.g. 'I am now less likely to travel'), on a scale from 1 ('never') to 5 ('always'). The sum of item scores was used. Cronbach's Alpha for this scale was 0.61.

Emotional stability was assessed in the 2014 wave only. Respondents completed the 10-item personality inventory (TIPI) (Gosling, Rentfrow and Swann, 2003). The emotional stability subscale consists of two items ('anxious, easily upset' and 'calm, emotionally stable'). The factor score was calculated and used as a measure of emotional stability/anxiety. The factor-score was used (rather than the sum-score) to avoid high levels of multicollinearity in the analyses in which the interaction between emotional stability and time was included. Given the fact that this subscale consists of only two items, using a mean-centred sum score of items would not lead to different results.

Technology optimism was measured in both 2014 and 2016 by the optimism subscale of the Abbreviated Technology Readiness Index (Victorino *et al.*, 2009), which is based on the Technology Readiness Scale (Parasuraman, 2000). This subscale has three items reflecting attitudes towards technology in daily life

70   *Hans Vermeersch* et al.

(e.g. 'Technology gives people more control over their daily lives') on a scale of 1 ('completely disagree') to 5 ('completely agree'). Cronbach's Alpha for this scale was 0.55 in 2014. Although this is low, corrected item-total correlations varied between 0.25 and 0.43. For this reason we will use this scale, but with caution. The sum of item scores was used.

Analyses

Group A allows us to directly analyse these individuals' change in attitudes over time, using a repeated measures design. To assess the differences in relationship strength between independent variables and acceptance of SOSTs in 2014 and 2016, a linear regression was used.

Group B allows us to analyse whether differences exist in mean scores on attitudes between Wave 2014 and Wave 2016, controlling for possible changes in the sociodemographic background of our student population, using a linear regression model. We used the following variables as control variables:

* Gender: male ('0'), female ('1')
* Age: age in years
* Parental SES: parental level of education scored '1' ('no primary education') to '5' ('education at university level'), averaged for maternal and paternal education
* Students' secondary school education: 'vocational', 'technical', 'general or arts'. Two dummy variables were created with 'general or arts' training as a category of reference.
* Student's educational programme: 'society and security', 'applied psychology', 'social educational care', 'social work'. Three dummy variables were created with 'social work' as a category of reference.

If both group and individual changes indicate similar trends, we have strong evidence that a real change in attitudes has taken place over the last year.

Subsequent analyses will be used to further validate that changes in attitudes can be attributed to the Paris attacks.

Results

Sample profile

Table 4.1 describes the profile of the panel that completed both waves (Group A) as well as the respondents that completed the survey in 2014 or 2016 (Group B).

On average, respondents were 20 years old when they completed the survey and over three quarters were female in both groups. This reflects departmental gender differences, as the specific Bachelor programmes on offer in the Department of Applied Social Studies tend to attract more female students.

Table 4.1 Sample profile

	Group A	Group B		Total
		2014	2016	
N	113	307	186	493
Gender				
Male	16.8%	27.0%	17.8%	23.5%
Female	83.2%	73.0%	82.2%	76.5%
Mean age	20.4	20.2	20.6	20.3
Bachelor's degree				
Society and security	16.8%	20.7%	19.7%	20.3%
Social work	28.3%	23.1%	27.9%	24.9%
Social educational care	31.9%	28.8%	26.2%	27.8%
Applied psychology	23.0%	27.4%	26.2%	27.0%

Source: author.

Changes in attitudes

In this section we look at whether students' attitudes changed between waves. We first look at whether opinions of individuals that completed both waves (Group A) changed, before comparing average attitudes across our independent samples (Group B).

Group A, repeated measures

Table 4.2 below shows panel respondents' average values on each variable of interest for 2014 and 2016, and the F-statistic for changes between these values.

No significant changes in acceptability of SOSTs or fear of crime were found. Attitudes towards the 'privacy–control trade-off' changed significantly between 2014 and 2016 towards favouring more government control ($F = 24.34$; $p < 0.001$), while risk perception increased too ($F = 9.78$; $p < 0.002$).

Table 4.2 Changes in attitudes between 2014 and 2016

(N = 113)	2014	2016	F-statistic	P<
SOSTs acceptability	15.67	15.18	0.99	0.322
Privacy–control trade-off	10.44	12.33	24.34	0.001
Trust in public authorities	16.70	16.75	0.01	0.917
Justice system	5.45	5.02	3.82	0.054
Risk perception	12.77	13.94	9.78	0.002
Fear of crime	9.19	8.80	1.23	0.271
Technology optimism	9.53	9.97	3.69	0.058

Source: author.

72 Hans Vermeersch et al.

Technology optimism increased significantly as well ($F=3.69$; $p<0.058$). While no significant change in trust in public authorities was found on average, a post-hoc analysis showed that trust in the judicial system in particular did decrease between 2014 and 2016.

Group B, means comparison

Table 4.3 shows average values of each variable for respondents that completed the questionnaire only in 2014 and those that only completed in 2016, the P values for a one-way ANOVA analysis of differences, as well as regression coefficients for the effects of 'wave' in a multivariate linear regression (controlling for demographic differences between the two samples) and their respective P values.

We found little effect of wave on acceptability of SOSTs ($r=-0.08$; $p<0.130$). The privacy–control trade-off, on the other hand, increased substantially; respondents in 2016 were significantly more likely to trade in privacy concerns for government control ($r=0.20$; $p<0.000$). As the above analyses on the panel data indicate, respondents seem to favour more control by the government, but appear more reluctant to do so when these technologies are made concrete. Average trust in public authorities has not changed dramatically, although a post-hoc analysis also shows a significant decline in average trust in the judicial system ($r=-0.13$; $p<0.024$) between the 2014 and 2016 wave. In line with an increase in risk perceptions among students that completed both waves, we also found an increase in risk perceptions between our independent samples ($r=0.09$; $p<0.093$). We observed few differences in fear of crime or technology optimism between waves.

Table 4.3 Average differences between 2014 and 2016, P values for differences (one-way ANOVA), effect of wave, controlling for demographic differences and respective P values

	2014	2016	P<	β wave[1]	P<
N	307	186			
SOSTs acceptability	15.73	15.07	0.179	−0.084	0.130
Privacy–control trade-off	11.19	12.73	0.000	0.202	0.000
Trust in public authorities	33.61	33.22	0.664	−0.061	0.280
Justice system	5.77	5.46	0.112	−0.131	0.020
Risk perception	12.94	13.51	0.097	0.094	0.093
Fear of crime	8.67	8.88	0.557	−0.006	0.909
Technology optimism	9.81	9.88	0.760	0.026	0.651

Source: author.

Note
1 Standardized linear regression coefficient controlling for gender, age, parental SES, high school education and current educational programme.

Post-hoc analyses

In this section we evaluate whether students' attitudes were affected by framing, or the events in Brussels in March 2016. Additional analyses look at whether changes in opinions are associated with terrorism, as well as at research question 2 – whether more anxious students responded differently to these events.

Terror frame and changes in attitudes after the Abdeslam arrest

Table 4.4 below shows average values for each of our variables in 2016, comparing respondents that were shown the terror frame to respondents in the control group. It also shows the results of a multivariate regression, using a dummy variable to evaluate the effects of this frame on each of the variables whilst controlling for demographic differences between these groups.

We do not observe any significant differences between these groups, on any of the variables of interest, suggesting the terror frame in itself did not substantially affect respondents' attitudes but indeed that more substantial changes took place in this population since 2014.

These findings are further corroborated when we distinguish between those that completed the survey before and after the Brussels events. Table 4.5 shows mean changes in the variables of interest, distinguishing between groups that completed the survey before the arrest of Salah Abdeslam, those that did thereafter and those that did after the Brussels attacks, as well as the regression coefficient of a dummy variable for this arrest.[4]

The arrest of Salah Abdeslam had no clear impact on attitudes towards the 'privacy–control trade-off' or any of the other variables. The small sample size, however, allows only for the detection of moderate to large changes in attitudes and precludes an assessment as to whether small changes have occurred. Because of the lack of statistical power it is impossible to assess whether the Brussels attacks (one week after Abdeslam's arrest) in themselves had an additional impact.

Table 4.4 Average differences between respondents that had a terror or control frame in 2016 and effect of this frame, controlling for demographic differences

	Terror frame	*Control*	β *terror frame*[1]	P<
N	*152*	*142*		
SOSTs acceptability	15.02	15.24	0.043	0.534
Privacy–control trade-off	12.51	12.75	0.027	0.707
Trust in public authorities	32.20	33.41	0.074	0.293
Risk perception	13.86	13.54	−0.045	0.523
Fear of crime	8.99	8.74	−0.029	0.652
Technology optimism	9.82	10.11	0.072	0.307

Source: author.

Note
1 Standardized linear regression coefficient controlling for gender, age, parental SES, high school education and current educational programme.

74 Hans Vermeersch et al.

Table 4.5 Average differences according to time of completion, and effect of arrest of Salah Abdeslam, controlling for demographic differences

	2014	2016			β Salah[1]	P<
		Before Salah	After Salah	After Brussels		
N	307	223	61	15		
SOSTs acceptability	15.72	15.16	14.80	15.79	−0.022	0.983
Privacy–control trade-off	11.19	12.73	12.30	12.23	−0.114	0.122
Trust in public authorities	33.61	32.93	32.12	32.46	−0.034	0.640
Risk perception	12.94	13.66	13.93	13.62	−0.030	0.681
Risk of terrorism	n/a	5.60	6.49	6.07	0.115	0.120
Fear of crime	8.67	8.85	9.14	8.38	−0.003	0.958
Fear of terrorism	n/a	2.45	2.85	2.47	0.104	0.158
Technology optimism	9.80	9.81	10.38	10.64	0.106	0.150

Source: author.

Note
1 Standardized linear regression coefficient controlling for gender, age, parental SES, high school education and current educational programme.

Nevertheless, these analyses support the idea that the change in attitudes resulted from the Paris events in 2015 and suggest that these attitudes were not dramatically altered, either by framing or the terror-related events that occurred later on in Belgium. The changes in the privacy–control trade-off as well as risk perceptions were already apparent before the Brussels events, and independent of whether they were framed in a terror context, suggesting they are indeed longer-term consequences of a year of terror. Of course, we cannot discount the potential effects of other events and changes that occurred during this year, but further evidence discussed in the next section suggests these changes are indeed related to perceptions of terrorism.

Is terror-related fear/risk perception in 2016 related to the change in attitudes between 2014 and 2016?

For the data gathering in 2016 (but not 2014) we had for a subsample of the panel ($N=46$) measures available on risk perception of terrorism and fear of terrorism (in addition to the risk perception of crime and fear of crime). Post-hoc analyses on these data give additional support to the idea that the changes in risk perception of crime and attitudes towards the 'privacy–control trade-off' between 2014 and 2016 are related to terror-related risk perception and fear of terrorism.

The change in 'non-terror-related risk perception' – a value for each individual computed by subtracting RP2016 from RP2014 – between 2014 and 2016 was associated with the risk perception of terrorism ($r=0.27$, $p<0.075$) and fear of terrorism ($r=0.48$, $p<0.003$) measured in Wave 2016. The change in 'non-terror-related fear of crime' between 2014 and 2016 was associated with the 'risk perception of terrorism' ($r=0.33$, $p<0.025$) and 'fear of terrorism' ($r=0.67$, $p<0.001$), indicating that those who were high on fear and risk perception in 2016 were those who changed their minds more dramatically between 2014 and 2016. Interestingly, 'fear of terrorism' ($r=0.34$, $p<0.045$) in Wave 2016 but not 'risk of terrorism' was associated with change in opinion on 'privacy–control trade-off'. As mentioned above, changes in acceptance of SOSTs between 2014 and 2016 were unrelated to any of these variables.

Summarizing, individuals who saw high risks of terror attacks or had more fear of these attacks in 2016 are those who changed most strongly in opinion between 2014 and 2016.

Changes in attitudes depending on anxious personality

The interaction (not in the Tables) between wave (2014/2016) and anxious personality (as a covariate) is significant ($F=4.16$; $p<0.045$), indicating that individuals with a more anxious, less emotionally stable personality have a significantly higher increase in risk perception between 2014 and 2016. We observed no difference in the privacy–control trade-off or acceptance of SOSTs, suggesting more anxious people are not more or less likely to support these policies. No other interactions between personality and wave were found.

Conclusion and discussion

In a sample of undergraduate students, we analysed whether the 2015 Paris attacks have changed attitudes with respect to opinions on the 'privacy–control trade-off' in general and the specific use of SOSTs by public authorities. Our analyses build on previous studies that have focused on post-attack attitudes towards security-enhancing measures, but go one step further by using unique survey data that include both pre- and post-attack observations, part of which can be analysed at the individual level and another part at group level.

The results of both types of analyses are consistent: respondents perceive higher risks – even risks that are not terror-related – in their direct environment (neighbourhood) and they are more inclined to support governmental control over privacy in the privacy–control trade-off in 2016 than they were in 2014. In the panel sample respondents were also more optimistic with respect to the use of technology in general than they were in 2014.

Importantly, however, we found that although the 'privacy–control trade-off' changed between 2014 and 2016, there were no changes in acceptance of the use of SOSTs by public authorities. Respondents were not more willing to accept CCTV, DNA-data files, RFID and/or behavioural profiling in 2016 than they were in 2014. This indicates that, while in general respondents favour more control even if this may affect their privacy compared to the 2014 wave, this

76 *Hans Vermeersch* et al.

does not mean that they are ready to accept concrete measures. This may suggest, in line with increasing evidence thereof, that a privacy–control trade-off is an overly simplified way to interpret public opinion on the acceptance of SOSTs.

One of the key findings of the SURPRISE project was just that the public would like to see increased privacy as well as security (i.e. not either/or), and that SOSTs should be implemented transparently and under strict legal guidelines in order to be acceptable and perceived to be effective. In this survey, we did not find changes in trust of public authorities generally; however, post-hoc analyses in both groups revealed that trust in the judicial system has decreased between 2014 and 2016. Trust in the judicial system was also strongly correlated with the acceptance of SOSTs, although this disappeared in a multivariate regression, including trust in authorities in general. Trust in the justice system and authorities charged with managing SOSTS may thus be crucial components when considering the acceptability of these technologies.

We observed clear changes in risk perceptions and towards favouring government control over privacy concerns that were not affected by framing in terms of terrorism or further terror events in Brussels, suggesting these changes can indeed be attributed to external shocks that occurred in 2015 and were hypothesized to have fundamentally changed the way we think about security. Nevertheless, it is difficult to separate the terror-related events during 2015–2016 from the public and political discourse on terror and radicalization as themes that dominated the year 2015. While there is evidence showing that the Paris attacks in themselves served as the shock effect that precipitated the shift in our respondents' opinions, it is reasonable to suggest that it might be one of the causes. A post-hoc analysis of a sub-sample of the panel showed that the change in 'non-terrorism-related' risk perception, fear of crime between 2014 and 2016, was strongly associated with the fear of terrorism (Wave 2016). This suggests that terrorist events may have affected opinions on 'crime in general' and indicates that the terror-related events may indeed have contributed to this change.

Furthermore, in addition to the finding that risk perception has increased between 2014 and 2016, we found – based on the panel data – that this increase is more pronounced for individuals who rated themselves as more anxious and less emotionally stable on the personal inventory (TIPI) completed in the 2014 wave, indicating that personality differences may play an important role in how the events are processed.

In all, our results add to a limited number of studies that have documented the effects of 'external shocks or threats' on citizens' attitudes with respect to civil liberties. Although the results show a relatively consistent pattern, several limitations may hinder the interpretation of the findings.

First, our study population consisted of undergraduate students. The data presented cannot be considered representative of the opinions of the Flemish population. Moreover, it remains uncertain how experience with and/or knowledge of technology, which may be higher/lower in other segments of the population, may have affected the results of this study. However, there is no reason to assume that the results of our study are 'typical' for our study population and are markedly different from the general population.

Second, while our analyses suggest that the change in attitudes was already noticeable before the arrest of Abdeslam and/or the Brussels attacks, we do not have enough evidence to conclude that one or both events may have further altered attitudes. Hypothetically one could argue that the Paris attacks in the beginning and at the end of 2015 created a shock effect, as these were the first major attacks in Europe after the Madrid and London bombings and the first in which citizens were randomly targeted with assault rifles. After the Paris attacks, there was a sense of inevitability that more attacks could follow.

Third, it remains to be seen how stable/short-lived the changes in attitudes are. Little research has evaluated the longer-term consequences of terror attacks. Given the current threats and public discourse on terror and anti-terror measures, there is no reason to suggest that these changes may be short-lived. Moreover, the fact that this survey was conducted a few months after the Paris attacks suggests they did indeed have longer-term effects on perceptions of security.

Summarizing, in a sample of undergraduate students, we found evidence that the Paris attacks influenced attitudes towards the privacy–control trade-off, but they did not affect acceptance of four specific SOSTs. Further studies should evaluate these findings in samples of the general population. Future research should also evaluate the effects of external threats on trust in authorities and the potentially mediating or mitigating effects of this trust on the acceptance of SOSTs. The distinction between cognitive and emotional responses to threats also deserves further attention; while this study suggests terrorism predominantly affects cognitive perceptions of risk, whether and how emotional responses to these events may further affect attitudes could be evaluated.

Appendix

Students were given the following vignettes regarding SOSTs before being asked to what extent, on a scale of 1 to 7, they agreed or disagreed with the use of this technology by public authorities.

Radio frequency identification

Radio frequency identification (identification through radio waves) is a technology that allows for reading information from a distance through a 'chip'. This chip can be built into objects (cars, laptops, clothing …). These objects, or people wearing the objects or chip, can then be tracked and identified from a distance through radio frequency identification. The European Union wants to make the use of these chips compulsory in vehicles. In this way it becomes possible to track and trace vehicles and to identify the owner of the vehicle from a distance.

78   *Hans Vermeersch* et al.

DNA-database

Some voices are calling for the establishment of a DNA-database for all Belgian residents. DNA (a person's genetic code) is unique for each individual. Through collecting this DNA in a database, when DNA is found in a certain place or on a certain object, it is possible to verify the 'identity' of its owner.

Smart CCTV

In many cities smart CCTV systems are in operation. Smart CCTV systems can 'recognize' license plates of vehicles, intercept conversations in the surrounding public space and/or warn operators in case of suspicious noise, words or shouting. Some smart CCTV can even recognize faces if these are collected in a database.

Behavioural profiling

New technologies allow for combining and connecting data from several data-bases on a large scale, making it relatively easy to establish 'profiles' of people or groups, based on preferences, tastes, behaviour and interests. This can be done, for instance, through combining data on a person's online behaviour with data on individual purchases, criminal records and convictions, medical data....

Trust in public authorities

How much do you trust ... (on a scale of 1 to 9)

The federal government (Belgian government)
The Flemish government
The local government (municipality)
The police
The intelligence services (e.g. Security of the State)
The judicial system

Privacy–control trade-off

To what extent do you agree or disagree with the following statements ... (on a scale of 1 to 5)

Public authorities should have increased access to personal information of individuals (including bank account information)
Public authorities should have more possibilities to tap telephone conversations
Public authorities should have more possibilities to intercept private internet conversations
Public authorities have too much power to monitor the lives of individuals
I'm concerned about the power public authorities have to follow our online behaviour

Risk perception

On a scale of 1 to 5, what risk do you have to become a victim in your neighbourhood of ...

Burglary
Aggression
Vandalism
Illegal dumping of waste
Bicycle theft

Fear of crime

On a scale of 1 to 5, how safe do you feel in your neighbourhood?

On a scale of 1 to 5, how often does it happen that ...
you avoid areas in your neighbourhood because you feel unsafe
you don't open the door for strangers because you feel unsafe
you avoid leaving the house after dark

Fear of terrorism

The past year 2015 was marked by terror attacks. Many of these attacks were claimed by the terror network of Islamic State, which attacked ever closer to 'home' and chose increasingly random targets. Think for instance of the attacks on Charlie Hebdo and a Jewish supermarket, beachgoers in Tunisia, and restaurant and concert-goers in Paris.

To what extent do you agree or disagree with the following statements ... (on a scale of 1 to 5)

I am now less likely to travel than I was before the attacks
I have adjusted my _____ since the attacks
I catch myself distrusting people with a clearly Muslim identity
I now feel less secure at large events and public places where many people gather together

On a scale from none to very large, how small or large do you perceive the risk that ...

A terror attack will occur in Europe
A terror attack will occur in Belgium
A terror attack will occur in Kortrijk
You, a friend or family member will become the victim of a terror attack

80   *Hans Vermeersch* et al.

Technology optimism

To what extent do you agree or disagree with the following statements ... (on a scale of 1 to 9)

Usually I can figure out myself how new high-technological products or services work, without help from others

New technology is usually too complex to be useful

I enjoy web shops because you are not limited by opening hours

When I need to get technical support from a distributor of a highly technological product or service, I sometimes feel 'exploited' by someone whom knows more than I do

Technology gives people more control over their daily lives

I don't think it's safe to pass on credit card details online

Generally, I'm one of the first people in my circle of friends to buy new technological gadgets as soon as they are available

I don't feel comfortable buying things in a shop that is only accessible online

Technology makes me more efficient in what I do

If you exchange information online, you can never be entirely sure it arrives at the right destination

Notes

1 These rates are based on end-of-year enrolment figures and do not take into account fluctuations throughout the year. The difference in response rates might be affected by the time of year; whereas students might be quite motivated at the start of the academic year in October–November, they experience a much heavier workload towards February–March. In addition, the educational system in Belgium encourages enrolment from a wide variety of backgrounds and educational levels, which is nevertheless reflected in high attrition rates. It is possible that the students that completed the second wave thus differ on average from those that completed the first. We control for any potential differences between the samples in our analyses of differences between waves (Group B).

2 Based on even/uneven birth dates.

3 The decision to assess these items in only half of the population was made to allow us to study whether the mere fact that respondents were asked questions about risks and fears about terrorism would affect their answers on other scales.

4 Respondents were scored 0 if they completed the questionnaire before the arrest and 1 thereafter.

References

Bozzoli, C. and Müller, C., 2011. Perceptions and attitudes following a terrorist shock: evidence from the UK. *European Journal of Political Economy*, 27, S89–S106.

Byrne, J. and Marx, G., 2011. Technological innovations in crime prevention and policing: a review of the research on implementation and impact. *Journal of Police Studies*, 20(3), pp. 17–40.

When it rains in Paris 81

Corbett, R. and Marx, G.T., 1991. Critique: no soul in the new machine: technofallacies in the electronic monitoring movement. *Justice Quarterly*, 8(3), pp. 399–414.

Davis, D.W. and Silver, B.D., 2004. Civil liberties vs. security: public opinion in the context of the terrorist attacks on America. *American Journal of Political Science*, 48(1), pp. 28–46.

Degli Esposti, S. and Gómez, E.S., 2015. Acceptable surveillance-orientated security technologies: insights from the SURPRISE project. *Surveillance & Society*, 13(3/4), p. 437.

Dragu, T., 2011. Is there a trade-off between security and liberty? Executive bias, privacy protections, and terrorism prevention. *American Political Science Review*, 105(1), pp. 64–78.

Echebarria-Echabe, A. and Fernández-Guede, E., 2006. Effects of terrorism on attitudes and ideological orientation. *European Journal of Social Psychology*, 36(2), pp. 259–265.

Friedewald, M., van Lieshout, M., Rung, S., Ooms, M. and Ypma, J., 2014. Privacy and security perceptions of European citizens: a test of the trade-off model. In: J. Camenish, S. Fischer-Hübner and M. Hansen, eds., *Privacy and identity management for the future internet in the age of globalisation*. Heidelberg: Springer, pp. 39–53.

Gosling, S.D., Rentfrow, P.J. and Swann, W.B., 2003. A very brief measure of the big-five personality domains. *Journal of Research in Personality*, 37(6), pp. 504–528.

Haubrich, D., 2003. September 11, anti-terror laws and civil liberties: Britain, France and Germany compared. *Government and Opposition*, 38(1), pp. 3–28.

Huddy, L., Feldman, S., Taber, C. and Lahav, G., 2005. Threat, anxiety, and support of antiterrorism policies. *American Journal of Political Science*, 49(3), pp. 593–608.

Lerner, J.S., Gonzalez, R.M., Small, D.A. and Fischhoff, B., 2003. Effects of fear and anger on perceived risks of terrorism a national field experiment. *Psychological Science*, 14(2), pp. 144–150.

Parasuraman, A., 2000. Technology Readiness Index (TRI): a multiple-item scale to measure readiness to embrace new technologies. *Journal of Service Research*, 2(4), pp. 307–320.

Patil, S., 2015. *Public perception of security and privacy: results of the comprehensive analysis of PACT's pan-European survey* [pdf]. Santa Monica, CA and Cambridge, UK: Rand Corporation. Available at: www.rand.org/content/dam/rand/pubs/research_reports/RR700/RR704/RAND_RR704.pdf [accessed on June 22, 2016].

Pavone, V. and Degli Esposti, S., 2010. Public assessment of new surveillance-oriented security technologies: beyond the trade-off between privacy and security. *Public Understanding of Science*, 21(5), pp. 556–572 (originally published online August 26, 2010).

Pavone, V., Degli Esposti, S. and Santiago, E., 2015. *D 2.4–key factors affecting public acceptance and acceptability of SOSTs* [pdf]. Seventh Framework Program. Available at: http://surprise-project.eu/wp-content/uploads/2015/02/SurPRISE-D24-Key-Factors-affecting-public-acceptance-and-acceptability-of-SOSTs-c.pdf [accessed on June 22, 2016].

Ponsaers, P., Devroe, E. and Meert, D., 2006. Tot de kern van de taak: het politionele kerntakendebat. *Orde van de dag: Criminaliteit en Samenleving*, 33, p. 55.

Posner, R.A., 2008. Privacy, surveillance, and law. *The University of Chicago Law Review*, 75(1), pp. 245–260.

Rountree, P.W. and Land, K.C., 1996. Perceived risk versus fear of crime: empirical evidence of conceptually distinct reactions in survey data. *Social Forces*, 74(4), pp. 1353–1376.

82 *Hans Vermeersch* et al.

Smith, H.J., Dinev, T. and Xu, H., 2011. Information privacy research: an interdisciplinary review. *MIS Quarterly*, 35(4), pp. 989–1016.

Solove, D.J., 2011. *Nothing to hide: the false tradeoff between privacy and security*. New Haven, CT: Yale University Press.

Straus, S., 2015. *Citizen summits on privacy, security and surveillance: synthesis report* [pdf]. Available at: http://surprise-project.eu/wp-content/uploads/2014/10/D6.3_Country_report_Germany_final_30.9.pdf [accessed on June 22, 2016].

Vermeersch, H. and De Pauw, E. 2017. The acceptance of new security oriented technologies: a 'framing' experiment. In: M. Friedewald, J.P. Burgess, J. Čas, R. Bellanova and W. Peissl, eds., *Surveillance, privacy and security: citizens' perspectives*. Abingdon, New York: Routledge, pp. 52–70.

Victorino, L., Karniouchina, E. and Verma, R., 2009. Exploring the use of the abbreviated technology readiness index for hotel customer segmentation. *Cornell Hospitality Quarterly*, 50(3), pp. 342–359.

Part II

Public and private decision-making

5 Securitization by regulation?

The Flemish mayor as democratic anchor of local security policies

Tom Bauwens[1]

Introduction

Security is arguably the most potent of all policy goals (Loader and Walker, 2007; Zedner, 2009; Stone, 2012). Within our modern social imaginary, the view prevails that security is the raison d'être of our liberal democratic governments. We hold these governments responsible for ensuring public order and security for the common good of all (Taylor, 2004). Invoking security can, however, be used to trump other societal values and introduce authoritarian measures that would ordinarily be politically untenable – especially when faced with insecurity in times of crises:

> During crises, leaders often claim that to ensure security, they must be able to act swiftly and forcefully, without the constraints on executive power that law is meant to exert. Invoking threats to security and public order, they declare a state of emergency and suspend ordinary laws, governmental procedures, and sometimes constitutions.
>
> (Stone, 2012, p. 152)

Defining social problems as issues of insecurity tends to invoke a special kind of politics, one that replaces normal politics of deliberation with an authoritarian politics of exception (Neocleous, 2008). The securitization of social practices, therefore, is never innocent. Besides seeing the state as a benevolent provider of security, it could also be seen as a standing threat. Some authors propose moral criteria to ensure a just securitization (Floyd, 2014) or recommend legal principles to curtail the pursuit of security (Zedner, 2009), while others suggest leaving the vocabulary altogether (see Neocleous and Rigakos, 2011). Confronted with this authoritarian threat to security, it seems obvious to regulate security in order to judge interventions in terms of their necessity, proportionality and pertinence, or look for alternative perspectives on public issues. But while ethicists and lawyers discuss the proper use of security in their ivory towers, local policy makers are confronted with the normative dilemmas of security in their day-to-day practice.

Grand principles, whether they are legal principles or moral standards, must always be translated into practical actions and balanced against a wider range of considerations. This is especially true when dealing with 'wicked' problems such as insecurity, where there is high uncertainty about the relevant knowledge claims, high preference volatility in opinion and even conflict about the values at stake (Hoppe, 2010, p. 73). In Belgium, the duty to assess the (in)security of particular situations and decide what ought to be done rests with the mayor. As elected politicians, they arguably ensure the democratic anchorage of local security policies. They have to account for their choices and could face electoral retribution if they do not succeed in taming insecurity. Not much is known, however, about how they ascribe meaning to this responsibility. In this contribution, I will present a heuristic framework that helps us to understand and explain how mayors in the Flemish region of Belgium experience their duty to provide security. My argument is that we should demystify the use of the concept 'security' before we regulate its use.

The local governance of security in Belgium

Cities have always been crucial in the provision of policing and security (Lippert and Walby, 2013). During the eighteenth century, the ideal of regulation and effective policing by local authorities in the interest of good order was common throughout Western and Central Europe. The growth of the nation-states that surrounded them led to restraining this urban independence (Lees and Lees, 2007), but some argue that the twenty-first century will be the century of cities once again:

> Today, after a long history of regional success, the nation-state is failing us on the global scale. It was the perfect political recipe for the liberty and independence of autonomous peoples and nations. It is utterly unsuited to interdependence. The city, always the human habitat of first resort, has in today's globalising world once again become democracy's best hope.
>
> (Barber, 2013, p. 3)

Local scales of government, like the municipality, are able not only to persist in the contemporary age of globalization, but are also acquiring new importance and powers (Valverde, 2012; Barber, 2013). Cities, and indeed municipalities, represent a level of governance sufficiently local to demand pragmatism and efficiency in problem solving but sufficiently networked to be able to fashion cooperative solutions to the interdependent challenges (Barber, 2013).

Within the state of Belgium, the municipality is the smallest administrative subdivision to have democratically elected representation.[2] Although they existed before the creation of Belgium in 1831, their number has by now dropped from 2739 to 589. Of those municipalities, 308 are within the Flemish region, the Dutch-speaking region in the north of Belgium. The regions are responsible for the administrative control over the municipalities with regard to the composition, the organization, the competences and the activities of the municipal institutions, which means that there are organizational and legal differences between the three regions. The focus of my research is on the municipalities within the region of Flanders (Bauwens, 2015). Municipalities are responsible for the collective needs of the inhabitants, and therefore have extensive powers to cover everything that is in the 'communal interest'. They are also mandated to perform the tasks imposed on them by higher authorities, such as keeping the registers of births, deaths and marriages and, importantly, maintaining public order and security. These local duties and competences in the field of crime control, prevention and security have been expanding over the last decades, a trend which is also noticeable in other jurisdictions (Edwards and Hughes, 2005; Schinkel, 2011). As the possibility of forestalling risks competes and even takes precedence over a traditional post-crime response (Zedner, 2007), procedures of the judicial system give way to preventive measures by governmental administrations. Local governments are increasingly identified as the optimal point of departure for establishing multi-agency security policies. In Belgium, the mayor in particular emerges as the embodiment of the aspiration to tackle (in)security at the municipal level (Bauwens *et al.*, 2011).

The daily administration of the municipality is taken care of by the college of mayor and aldermen, who are typically selected by the municipal council among its members.[3] The mayor holds the most important local political office and acts as the public figurehead of the municipality. The mayoral duties include local competences (for the 'communal interest') as well as entrusted responsibilities and tasks (for the 'general interest'). This includes the legal duty to provide order and security for its inhabitants. In his capacity as chief of the 'administrative police', he has a privileged relation with the emergency services and the public prosecutor's office, and even has the legal authority to take all necessary measures to maintain public order and security in his municipality. He embodies the unifying link between these various domains, organizations and structures related to security, and is therefore often appointed as the 'director' of the local security policy. The mayor therefore has an important role in defining what insecurity entails, which security measures are to be introduced in practice and how these are implemented (Bauwens *et al.*, 2011). But how these locally elected politicians interpret and experience this demanding duty, how they understand and delimit the concept of (in)security and how they (re)define their role accordingly remains underdeveloped.

Understanding the experience of having to provide security

Defining (in)security is notoriously difficult. The imprecision of the term has allowed a plethora of measures and policies to be justified in its name. It has been deployed inconsistently and widely across a range of spaces and contexts. Policies meant to generate security must also create it in the psychological sense. It is not merely about the absence of danger, but also the absence from the *worry* about danger (Stone, 2012). Significant differences in perceptions and tolerance of threats, ordering practices and patterns of social cohesion shape local perceptions and influence its (political) mobilization to define situations as '(in)secure'.

88 *Tom Bauwens*

As a consequence, it has been used to refer to everything from anxieties about crime, unemployment, financial uncertainty and personal health to concerns at the international level about the dangers of climate change, population growth and terrorism (Zedner, 2009). The growing concern about this upward spiral of security has led some scholars to declare themselves against security (Neocleous and Rigakos, 2011).

(In)security is thus a classical 'wicked' problem that can arguably never be solved, but only temporarily settled. It is defined in an *institutional void*, where there are no clear and generally accepted rules and norms according to which politics is to be conducted and policy measures are to be agreed upon (Hajer, 2009). Different experts might provide different advice, all of which might be based on legitimate concerns and provide a sensible interpretation of the situation (Hoppe, 2010). This results in a series of complex negotiations with a variety of stakeholders and claims-makers about how to understand the problem and what can be done about it. It is less about the identification and analysis of objective social threats, and more about the authoritative enactment of meaning (Hajer, 2009). According to Marianne Valverde (2011), it is therefore unproductive to think about security used as a noun as if it designated an entity. She argues that we should not think about security as a thing, concept or condition, but rather as an umbrella term under which one can see a multiplicity of governance processes that are dynamic and internally contradictory: 'all we can know about security is what people do in its name' (Valverde, 2011, p. 5).

The purpose of my research was to understand and explain how Flemish mayors deal with this complexity and ascribe meaning to (in)security (Bauwens, 2015). Instead of assuming that an objective understanding of this process can be developed, my epistemological point of departure is on the fundamentally practical and social nature of understanding, which is always something more than re-creating someone else's meaning. Understanding is not a reconstruction, but rather a productive (co)construction of meaning. This results in what Hans-Georg Gadamer (2013) would describe as a 'fusion of horizons'. Since it is often assumed that our own horizon, the historically conditioned experiential space that guides our gaze onto the world, constrains our understanding of others, attempts are often made to nullify the researchers' bias and prejudice during the data collection process, for example by bracketing (i.e. 'temporary suspending') a priori knowledge. But our situatedness and individual perspectives arguably also *enable* our understanding of the other. Knowledge is not produced through disembodied reason, but by people within a historically situated context (Bauwens and Luyten, 2015). Indeed, my background knowledge, disciplinary tradition and personal interest serve as a prerequisite to understanding the other. Instead of trying to ignore my presumptions or temper my interests, I literally brought them to the field.

My research entailed carrying out interviews with seventeen Flemish mayors, upon which the following insights are based. During these conversations, I explored the depth and breadth of (in)security as a phenomenon and report on its place as a local policy domain within the local government, administration and

Securitization by regulation? 89

emergency services. I invited the mayors to share and interpret their own experiences by introducing a selection of newspaper articles. This technique encouraged them to give tangible examples, but also kept our conversation on track to cover the topics I was interested in. I examined how the mayors assess the state of security in their municipality and reflect on their own role in its provision. I was always aware that politicians tend to be ambiguous and vague during interviews – especially when it concerns a topic as delicate as security. In order to avoid institutional talk and textbook answers, I presented myself as an 'expert' (Rhodes, 't Hart and Noordegraaf, 2007), having knowledge of the institutional organization and complexities of the local safety and security policies. I was not interested in how well the mayors were able to explain and defend their security policy, but rather how they experience it, what difficulties and challenges arise and so on.

The analysis of these exchanges led to the identification of three distinctive interpretative repertoires – clusters of terms, categories and metaphors drawn upon to characterize and evaluate actions and events (Potter and Wetherell, 1987) – that the mayors used to make sense of security: a technocratic repertoire of policy, an expressive repertoire of responsiveness and a judicial repertoire of justice. These repertoires provide the mayor with a point of reference, criteria, strategies and rhetoric to give meaning to security. The main characteristics of these repertoires are summarized in Table 5.1 below.

Within *the interpretative repertoire of policy*, the mayors position themselves as the conductor of the governance of security. From a central but distant position, he or she oversees the local municipality, defines the general strategy and monitors the interplay between the different actors and organizations involved. The vocabulary is technocratic, concise and rational. Security, then, is the result of an effective and efficient local organization. Within *the repertoire of responsiveness*, in contrast, tangible issues of insecurity and unsafety are at the forefront. The mayors are identified as the father or mother figure with close ties with the local residents and are committed to fulfilling their expectations. They want to react fast and pragmatically to the individualized interests of the citizens. The performativity and expressivity of policy interventions are emphasized. Finally, within *the repertoire of justice* ('rechtsstaat'), the mayors emphasize their attributed role as officer of the administrative police, responsible for guarding the general interest and taking all necessary measures to maintain public order. From this independent position, they supervise the legitimacy and lawfulness of claims, while at the same time considering fairness and justice (Bauwens, 2015).

To be sure, these positions and their associated repertoires do not refer to distinctive types of mayors. They represent three sets of dynamic resources used by all the mayors to cope with the ambiguity of security and its plurality of meanings. The repertoires are not mutually exclusive; there is a complicated relationship between them, which allows mayors to rely on them in order to assess the situation and justify their interventions. Crucially, this is done out of an unassailable drive to provide solutions for the problems they are confronted with.

Table 5.1 Overview of the interpretative repertoires

	Policy repertoire	*Responsiveness repertoire*	*Rule of law/state of justice repertoire*
Subject position	*'Conductor'* Distant	*'Father/mother figure'* Committed	*'Guardian of the general interest'* Independent
Point of reference	Municipal interest Local government	Individualized interest Personal relations	Public order General interest
Criteria	Effectiveness Efficiency	Expressivity Performativity	Legitimacy and lawfulness Justice and fairness
Strategy	Proactive Concise and technical	Reactive Engagement	Procedural Critical
Rhetoric	Logos	Pathos	Ethos

Source: Bauwens, 2015, p. 233.

The prohibition to party as an innovative security practice

This solutions-focused intentionality contributes to the creation of innovative security practices, such as the so-called 'prohibition to party' (Bauwens, 2015, pp. 193–194). I encountered this peculiar security measure as an idiosyncratic local effort to protect local parties from known troublemakers by banning them from the vicinity.

One of the mayors explained that he was confronted with a handful of individuals who cause a lot of problems, particularly by stirring up fights at local parties. Although their identity is well known by the authorities, it proved to be difficult to get them prosecuted by the penal system. Something had to be done and a local response seemed to be the only way to combat impunity. This led to the creation of zonal bans on individuals who are known for disturbing the peace. This policy did not receive a lot of (national) attention, but other municipalities who were faced with similar problems nonetheless adopted it. The city of Kortrijk took this policy one step further and developed a project called 'safe party zones'.[4] Whereas the original prohibition to attend parties relied on the organizers or local police officials to recognize the individuals and effectively enforce the ban, the 'safe party zones' automatized this process. Safe party zones are local events, organized by recognized youth associations, whereby every visitor's digital identification card is scanned upon entry. The system was approved by the Belgian Privacy Commission, which means that the organizers are not actually reading or registering personal information, but merely checking whether the person is registered as being 'banned'. Such individuals are effectively denied access to the event. The prohibition of partying applies to all youth-related events that are affiliated with this project, making it a targeted, localized system. It is clear, however, that the prohibition of partying also institutes mass surveillance practices. Recently, the city of Lier adopted a similar system called 'safe zones', expanding the scope of the system to pubs and events for the general public.[5]

Notice that these mayoral measures are not meant to sanction individual behaviour, but to avoid or to stop public disorder and protect the community. When the city of Antwerp tried to introduce zonal bans in 2009 to tackle anti-social behaviour in the Antwerp Red Light District, the League of Human Rights successfully indicted this measure. The Council of State[6] (which is the supreme administrative court in Belgium) confirmed that municipalities are allowed to take all necessary measures for the protection of public security and order, but judged that the zonal ban in Antwerp was conceived of as a municipal administrative sanction. Since the list of possible administrative sanctions within the Federal law on municipal administrative sanctions was exhaustive and did not include zonal bans, it could not be adopted by the municipal council (Schram and Lievens, 2015, p. 297). The prohibition of partying is therefore not a sanction, but legally founded on the administrative police powers of the mayor, which allow him to take all necessary measures to maintain public order and security. The mayors have the discretion to decide what kind of action is appropriate. In this case, the individual bans are legitimized with the argument that they are necessary to protect the inhabitants, the local youth, against the outbreak of fights at parties. One of the mayors involved in my research recognized that these kinds of policies probe the legal boundaries of their competences. But while one of the mayors was in favour of regulating this practice by explicitly incorporating individual zonal bans in the municipal law, others were reluctant to accept this idea:

> There are two reasons why I think this should not be done. First of all, we must be careful with these kinds of measures because of the democratic impact. And secondly ... we can already instigate these bans. So.... Let's not introduce them in the law. We ought to be careful. But at the same time ... I would use them if I had to.

One year after this interview, in 2013, the federal parliament included zonal banning in the municipal law as exceptional measures of administrative police.[7] From a rule-of-law point of view, the inclusion of this specific policing measure in the municipal law seems to be a positive development. By explicitly introducing this measure in the municipal law, it was pulled out of the mayoral discretion. Terms and conditions are now more specifically defined. The ban is restricted to a period of one month, but is renewable two times; it cannot entail the municipality in its entirety and must be confirmed by the college of mayor and aldermen. A prior written warning is also mandatory, except in the case of needing to maintain public order.

The regulation of these zonal bans arguably contributes to more procedural justice by curtailing the potentially arbitrary exercise of the mayors' general policing powers. But whilst setting constraints, these rules are simultaneously suggesting new possibilities.

Securitization by regulation

In his book *The new democracy*, the Dutch sociologist Willem Schinkel (2012) notices how the legal possibilities of local governments to maintain public order and security are expanding. He warns that cities are becoming laboratories for innovative techniques of repression, fuelled by pragmatic populism and legitimized under the guise of security (Schinkel, 2012, pp. 327–328). The institutionalization of zonal bans in the municipal might seem to confirm Schinkel's fear of emerging repressive local policies via innovative security practices. The effective enforcement of the ban necessitates mass surveillance and promotes the idea that public order can be maintained by excluding individual troublemakers. But more importantly, the institutionalization of these individual zonal bans reinforces the mayor's role as provider of solutions and endorses the possible use of the mayoral exceptional policing powers. It normalizes exceptional security measures by effectively establishing them as an instrument in the mayors' toolbox. Regulation seems to lead to securitization.

Securitization by regulation? 93

To be sure, the use of mayoral exceptional policing measures was already regulated. Not only must administrative police measures obey the rules set by the European Court of Human Rights – they must be in accordance with the law and necessary in a democratic society – but they must also obey the general principles of good governance that moderate the governmental practice: they must be in proportion, extensively motivated, preferably preceded by a hearing and in accordance with higher norms and regulations. But replacing these general standards with specific principles or more narrowly tailored, objective rules does not eliminate the subjectivity and discretion in their application (Valverde, 2012, p. 69).

Just as I doubt the feasibility of abolishing the concept of security (Neocleous and Rigakos, 2011), I'm not convinced that additional regulation of the use of the term by establishing judicial (Zedner, 2009) or normative (Floyd, 2014) criteria will resolve how security will be used in practice. Regulation fails to take into account how mayors establish the meaning of security in practice. The regulation of zonal bans fuels the legal repertoire of mayors, but without taking their other repertoires into account or challenging the underlying solutions-based intentionality. At first sight, a solutions-focused intentionality might seem to be a good attitude towards (in)security. After all, it is better to light a candle than curse the darkness. But one of the mayors in my research bluntly admitted that she had never taken the time to really think about the causes of insecurity in her municipality, despite the fact that she had been talking about her policing responsibility and defending her security measures for over half an hour. The focus of the mayor often remains on the tip of the iceberg – solutions or possible alternatives – but the vast part below the water surface is ignored: the way problems arise and are represented (Hoppe, 2010). The interpretative repertoires the mayors rely on to make sense of security already provide a strong foundation from which to approach the emergence of problems from different perspectives. Political behaviour is, of course, a complicated mix of self-seeking, self-interest and broader, higher aims (Reeher, 2006). For politicians who are dependent on popular support, it is reasonable to think that short-term benefits will regularly trump long-term sustainable goals. A degree of suspicion about the motivation and behaviour of politicians is therefore a healthy component to a vigorous democracy. I am, however, optimistic about the possibilities of politics and its commitment to stability and compromise through social dialogue (Flinders, 2012). My research shows that mayors do not simply concede to popular demands, perform cost-benefit calculations or blindly apply formal legal rules. By combining elements from different repertoires, they take the particularities and complexities of the situation into account, typically by drawing upon their relationships with relevant others, citizens and policy advisers.

Conclusion

(In)security is not an abstract puzzle waiting to be solved through the application of principles and procedures, but rather an ever-present challenge to be negotiated. Local governments – and especially the local mayors – find themselves at the forefront in this quest. They are appointed 'director' of the local security policy and are expected to assess situations and take all necessary measures to maintain security. Given the extensive authority the concept of security entails, it seems logical to formally regulate its use. But I have argued that the use of the concept should be demystified first.

My research into Flemish mayors revealed that they rely on three interpretative repertoires – clusters of terms, categories and metaphors drawn upon to characterize and evaluate actions and events (Potter and Wetherell, 1987) – to make sense of (in)security: a technocratic repertoire of policy, an expressive repertoire of responsiveness and a judicial repertoire of justice. These repertoires allow the mayors to create arguments and justify their interventions. They are deployed especially in order to provide solutions. As an example, I presented the prohibition of partying as an innovative local security practice. This measure emerged as a creative interpretation of the mayor's legal competence in order to solve the problems posed by individual troublemakers, but the practice was eventually regulated and added to the municipal law as a specific local policing measure. Regulation fails to consider the fact that the law is only one of the resources used by the mayors to make sense of (in)security. The introduction of the legal possibility does not mean that mayors will actually use the measure as it is intended to be used. Mayors are also responsive to participatory input and keen to provide effective and efficient public service output. It does, however, contribute to the process of securitization, the societal tendency to approach social problems from a perspective of security. Even if those regulations entail protections for individuals against governmental intervention, they reinforce the public's expectations towards the mayor 'to do something' on the one hand and the mayoral urge to produce solutions on the other.

The challenge remains to transcend the mayors' solutions-focused intentionality to include considerations about the underlying problems to be addressed. The mayor's considerations should include not only the weighing of possible solutions, but also the search for, debating and evaluation of competing representations of problems. To label social issues as insecurity is not a neutral or technical exercise, but demands normative considerations. As elected representatives of the people, mayors could ensure the democratic anchorage of this process.

Notes

1 Postdoctoral researcher at the research group Crime & Society (CRiS), Vrije Universiteit Brussel (tom.bauwens@vub.ac.be).
2 Except for the nine districts in the municipality of Antwerp, a sub-municipal administrative entity with an elected council.
3 Their assignments and the formation of governmental majorities are subject to party-political bargaining. The largest party wins office and typically the number of preferential votes collected by certain candidates will determine individual appointments (Wayenberg, De Rynck, Steyvers and Pilet, 2011).
4 See www.kortrijk.be/safepartyzone.
5 See www.safezones.be.

6 Council of State, 23 October 2009, judgment no 197.212.
7 Confusingly, they were added in the slipstream of the law on municipal administrative sanctions. To be sure, zonal bans were not defined as an administrative sanction, but as an exceptional measure of administrative police (art.134sexies New Municipal Law). The Constitutional Court has endorsed this reasoning. Taking administrative measures, including zonal banning, to protect the population from future infringements is in accordance with the rule of law.

References

Barber, B., 2013. *If mayors ruled the world*. New Haven, CT and London: Yale University Press.

Bauwens, T., 2015. *De burgemeester als regisseur van het lokale veiligheidsbeleid?* Den Haag: Boom Lemma Uitgevers.

Bauwens, T. and Luyten, I., 2015. *Experiencing experience: killing the researcher?* Paper presented at Experiencing Justice, Sint-Gillis.

Bauwens, T., Enhus, E., Ponsaers, P., Reynaert, H. and Van Assche, J., 2011. *Integraal veiligheidsbeleid tussen pragmatisme en idealisme. Het complexe samenspel van lokale en bovenlokale bestuurlijke actoren*. Brussels: VUBpress.

Edwards, A. and Hughes, G., 2005. Comparing the governance of safety in Europe: a geo-historical approach. *Theoretical Criminology*, 9(3), pp. 345–363.

Flinders, M., 2012. *Defending politics: why democracy matters in the twenty-first century*. Oxford: Oxford University Press.

Floyd, R., 2014. Just and unjust desecuritization. In: T. Balzacq, ed., *Contesting security*. London: Routledge.

Gadamer, H.G., 2013. *Truth and method* (Transl. J. Weinsheimer and D.G. Marshall). London: Bloomsbury Academic.

Hajer, M., 2009. *Authoritative governance: policy-making in the age of mediatization*. Oxford: Oxford University Press.

Hoppe, R., 2010. *The governance of problems: puzzling, powering, participation*. Bristol: The Policy Press.

Lees, A. and Lees, L.H., 2007. *Cities and the making of modern Europe, 1750–1914*. Cambridge: Cambridge University Press.

Lippert, R.K. and Walby, K., 2013. *Policing cities: urban securitization and regulation in a 21st century world*. London: Routledge.

Loader, I. and Walker, N., 2007. *Civilizing security*. Cambridge: Cambridge University Press.

Neocleous, M., 2008. *Critique of security*. Edinburgh: Edinburgh University Press.

Neocleous, M. and Rigakos, G.S. eds., 2011. *Anti-security*. Ottawa: Red Quill Books.

Potter, J. and Wetherell, M., 1987. *Discourse and social psychology: beyond attitudes and behaviour*. London: SAGE Publications.

Reeher, G., 2006. *First person political: legislative life and the meaning of public service*. New York: New York University Press.

Rhodes, R., 't Hart, P. and Noordegraaf, M. eds., 2007. So what? The benefits and pitfalls of being there. In: R. Rhodes, P. 't Hart and M. Noordegraaf, eds., *Observing government elites: up close and personal* (First edition). London: Palgrave Macmillan. pp. 206–233.

Schinkel, W., 2011. Prepression: the actuarial archive and new technologies of security. *Theoretical Criminology*, 15(4), pp. 365–380.

Schinkel, W., 2012. *De nieuwe democratie*. Amsterdam: De Bezige Bij.

Schram, F. and Lievens, J., 2015. *Gemeentelijke administratieve sancties. Een antwoord op overlast?* Brugge: Vanden Broele.

Stone, D., 2012. *Policy paradox: the art of political decision making*. New York: W.W. Norton & Company.

Taylor, C., 2004. *Modern social imaginaries*. Durham, NC: Duke University Press.

Valverde, M., 2011. Questions of security: a framework for research. *Theoretical Criminology*, 15(1), pp. 3–22.

Valverde, M., 2012. *Everyday law on the street: city governance in an age of diversity*. Chicago, IL: University of Chicago Press.

Wayenberg, E., De Rynck, F., Steyvers, K. and Pilet, J.-B., 2011. Belgium: a tale of regional divergence? In: J. Loughlin, F. Hendriks, and A. Lidström, eds., *The Oxford handbook of local and regional democracy in Europe*. New York: Oxford University Press.

Zedner, L., 2007. Pre-crime and post-criminology? *Theoretical Criminology*, 11(2), pp. 261–281.

Zedner, L., 2009. *Security*. London: Routledge.

6 Raising the flag

The state effects of public and private security providers at East Jerusalem's national parks

Lior Volinz

Introduction

There are a few surprising commonalities to be found between national parks and public security provision: both are determined and regulated by the state, and established to maintain order and guarantee (equal) access to a public good, whether it be the right to one's life and property or the maintenance of the country's natural and cultural wonders. In occupied East Jerusalem, the conflation of both promotes violence and further tensions as both state and non-state actors use national parks to displace (Palestinian) residents from their home and transform the space into a (Israeli) tourist attraction. Focusing on the practices employed by public and private security agents deployed at East Jerusalem's national parks, this chapter engages the concept of security performance to contribute to the debate on state effects and the assertion of graduated sovereignty.

Drawing from ethnographic fieldwork conducted in East Jerusalem, this chapter examines the case of Wadi Hilweh/City of David National Park. In examining the different performances by the variety of security actors active in and around this site, I argue that it is through daily practices employed by Israeli security personnel at national parks in East Jerusalem that state effects are (re)produced in contested locales. In developing the contention of Trouillot, Hann and Krti (2001) that state effects are 'increasingly obtained in sites other than the national, but that never fully bypass the national order', I aim to explore how Israel, the occupying state in East Jerusalem, is able to assert its sovereignty through security modalities, practices and encounters by having 'boots on the ground' in the form of public and private security.

Crafting the state

This chapter deals with the deeds (and misdeeds) of the state and its associated security actors; yet how should we conceptually approach the state – how can we confine the idea of the state to a form distinguishable from its individual institutions albeit removed from the larger society? Abrams (1988) noted that in examining the practices of the state, many scholars risk reification of the state as a 'state idea', which obfuscates the power relations embedded within the state.

98　*Lior Volinz*

The state is always an arena of struggle, one in which different actors strive for legitimacy, influence and domination, rather than an entity that by itself holds independent agency. The state thus always remains elusive to research, its edges fuzzy and its core in constant flux. Mitchell (1999) proposes to focus instead on state effects – the mundane material and social practices of a seemingly abstract structure. Such an approach requires attention to the practices and performances that compose state effects. This chapter follows the visualities, materialities and daily practices in which the state is performed by different security actors.

Building upon practice theory (Giddens, 1979; Ortner, 2006), I seek to explore the relations between structures and practices – namely, how is the state performed through security practices? Or correspondingly, how do security practices contribute to the reconfiguration of emerging pluralized and privatized security structures? I thus approach these relations from both the 'bottom' – in attending to street-level practices and materialities – and from the 'top', as constituted by novel public–private security structures. In attending to both practice and structure, I draw attention to the plurality of state and non-state security actors present in the city. In Jerusalem, as in other parts of the world, the protection of people and property is decreasingly an exclusive function of the public police force, and is increasingly maintained by a plethora of public and private security bodies (Loader, 1999).

Hansen (2006) turns to the case of pluralized security provision in post-apartheid South Africa to suggest that both public and private security actors engage in law-making violence, a task previously considered within the exclusive domain of the state. He proposes that the disciplinary and punitive practices of non-state security personnel represent a new sovereignty arising from the community and largely condoned by the state. In other words, when state actors are officially (politically and/or legally) limited in pursuing a controversial yet popular security policy, other actors come to the fore and indirectly, informally, yet under the consent of the state, implement such a policy. Hansen was working in the context of punitive and racially biased measures against people of colour. In this chapter, I focus on the practices employed by a plurality of security actors – police, military, border police and private security personnel in national parks in and around Jerusalem. I suggest that a similar condition exists in East Jerusalem, where a state-led project of Judaizing East Jerusalem, limiting Palestinian growth and dispossessing Palestinian residents of their property is pursued by a number of public and private security actors, who share, develop and divide the mundane practices of the Israeli state sovereignty performance in Occupied East Jerusalem's national parks.

The claims for sovereignty can be located within an arena of contestation – different actors aim to accommodate their stakes and compete successfully in the realm of governance, law and the monopoly over violence. Ong (2000) extended our understanding of 'graduated sovereignty' to reflect how states interact with the market and stratify the population in the allocation of resources and rights. Yet sovereignty is also contested outside the realm of the state, with other actors (global and local, public and private) competing with or complementing the state's claim on exclusive sovereignty. Sovereignty is constituted by the totality of its claimants; performative claims transgress the national state within and without national borders (Stepputat, 2015). The sovereignty performances by private security guards have also sparked an intensive scholarly discussion (Havkin, 2014; Goldstein, 2015) that analyses the outsourcing of security provision through a critical lens, which questions both the state's monopoly over violence and its significance in the neoliberal era.

Methodology

In the following pages, I explore the roles and practices of security agents at Wadi Hilweh/City of David National Park, located within a Palestinian neighbourhood in close proximity to Jerusalem's Old City. I've conducted participant observation – the collection of data through my own participation and observation of phenomena – in this site and other national parks in and around East Jerusalem during my fieldwork from February to September 2015. This method entailed long hours of observation in different capacities – as a guest of local families, as a visitor to the national park or as a participant in the neighbourhood's public events. I additionally include data from semi-structured interviews with different residents and security agents at these sites, conducted over the same period. Furthermore, I've conducted participatory transects with local residents around the neighbourhood. Participatory transects are a technique of systematically walking together with research respondents through a delimited area, in which the researcher asks for explanation of every space and structure along the way (Russell, 2012). By conducting these transects in areas of friction, such as in neighbourhoods facing expulsion or dispossession, I was able to get a better understanding of the site – including the number and type of homes under threat – as well as to collect valuable data related to security policies and practices as perceived by local residents. I subsequently analysed these same practices, both witnessed and reported on, as contributing to state effects that perform graduated sovereignty in contested locales. To preserve the security of my research collaborators and their families, their names and some identifying details were, when necessary, anonymized.

Apart from ethnographic fieldwork, I used several secondary sources, including protocols of legal proceedings, news reports, policy papers by nongovernmental organizations and parliamentarian protocols. These sources were cited and analysed in order to shed light on the composition and operation of the security provision in East Jerusalem, including the different practices and performances employed in and around the city's national parks.

Jerusalem, a divided city

The protracted hostilities in Israel-Palestine have brought continuous scholarly attention to the security operations, innovations and practices employed by the Israeli security actors in maintaining public order within Israel, as well as the

Israeli occupation in the West Bank, East Jerusalem and the Gaza Strip (see Konopinski, 2009; Dumper, 2013; Grassiani, 2013; Havkin, 2014). The case of East Jerusalem is of particular interest – a large agglomeration of neighbourhoods, villages, holy sites and a refugee camp under occupation by the Israeli authorities since 1967. Unlike the rest of the West Bank, East Jerusalem was officially annexed to Israel.[1] Jerusalemite Palestinian inhabitants were not granted Israeli citizenship, but were instead defined legally as stateless permanent residents of Israel, a precarious status which may later be revoked. East Jerusalem's administration was delegated to the Israeli civil authorities and not to the military. Therefore, East Jerusalem is substantially different from the rest of the Occupied Palestinian territories – in Jerusalem there is only one legal system for Palestinians and Israeli-Jewish residents: the Israeli control (and its associated illegal settlement project) persists under civilian authority and the police replaces the military in maintaining Israeli sovereignty and law over the occupied city.

Yet the mere military takeover and subsequent legal annexation of East Jerusalem does not denote the transformation of all of Jerusalem into 'Israeli territory'. Indeed, the city continues to be divided between Jewish-Israeli and Palestinian spaces, with a string of visible and invisible boundaries bisecting the city (Pullan *et al.*, 2007). Israeli-Jewish pupils follow the Israeli curriculum, while Palestinian pupils largely follow the Palestinian Authority curriculum; the Palestinian residents subscribe to their own electrical company and use their own public transport lines, while the Israeli-Jewish residents enjoy improved services with large governmental subsidies. The Israeli authorities continue their efforts to normalize, legitimize and entrench the Israeli sovereignty over East Jerusalem. Despite applying brute force, sanctions and incentives, the Israeli occupation continues to encounter stiff resistance from the city's Palestinian residents.

In this context, national parks, archaeological sites and green areas emerge as an important part of the toolbox of the Israeli authorities in asserting Israeli sovereignty in East Jerusalem since the occupation of 1967. While there are indeed many sites of cultural, historical and natural value around Jerusalem, national parks are established and developed in a manner which affects Palestinian residents of East Jerusalem unequally. Parks and archaeological sites are used to displace (and replace) Palestinian residents in the guise of conservation,[2] to establish tourist attractions for domestic and foreign audiences, to limit Palestinian construction and hinder urban expansion plans on their private land. Each of these sites becomes a base for security operations by the Israeli authorities – police stations are built within national parks, private security guards establish their presence around the sites' perimeters and enhanced enforcement of Israeli law and municipal regulations takes place under the green banners of the Israeli Nature and Parks Authority. Rassem Khamisi, a Palestinian Urban and Regional Planner, aptly described the reactions among Palestinians regarding the establishment of national parks on their land: 'They [Israeli urban planners] colour the map in green, which for the Palestinians means black' (Khamisi, 2015).

Private security and the Valley of Sweet Water

Hussam sat, as he often does, on a white plastic chair outside his cousin's tiny grocery shop in the Palestinian neighbourhood of Silwan, East Jerusalem. Customers come and go – women picking up groceries for the weekend meals, children getting some sweets and young men asking for cigarettes from behind the counter. Hussam occasionally works for his cousin, whose store is in the same street where they both reside, a long narrow road that ascends to the Old City's Dung Gate. I join him on another day that he spends chatting away by the side of the road, taking care of the occasional customer. The houses on this street are a mix of Palestinian homes with large back yards with the occasional olive tree, and Jewish-Israeli settlers' houses with large fences, security watchtowers equipped with one-sided mirrors, Israeli flags on the rooftops and CCTV cameras. Having just turned 50, Hussam has little memory of the days prior to the Israeli occupation of the city in 1967; he does, however, remember well the days prior to the massive arrival of Israeli-Jewish settlers in his part of Silwan, a neighbourhood called Wadi Hilweh. 'It used to be very quiet here', he said, while facing the congested street with racing vehicles and high-pitched sirens.

The City of David, established in 1970, has been declared an Israeli archaeological site; it is a part of the Jerusalem Walls National Park, which encompasses the entire area surrounding the Old City of Jerusalem. The Israeli Nature and Parks Authority has delegated the operation of the City of David site, in the neighbourhood of Wadi Hilweh ('The Valley of Sweet Water' in Arabic), to the Israeli-Jewish settlers association, Elad. The same organization is concurrently working on settling Israeli Jews in Wadi Hilweh, replacing or displacing Palestinian families through a series of expropriations and contested purchases aided by Israeli state bodies (Pullan and Gwiazda, 2009). Archaeology and its conservation and presentation in nature and heritage sites could provide a viable alternative to nationalist and ethnocentric readings of history. Instead, Greenberg (2009) argues that the Wadi Hilweh/City of David National Park provides an example for an exclusionist archaeology used within the context of a national conflict to displace and marginalize the local population. Pullan and Gwiazda (2009) contend that at the City of David site, an entire neighbourhood of Jerusalem was reconfigured as part of a particular, state-sponsored ideological and hegemonic project, adding that such transformation is closely related to the privatization of the site management, supervision and security provision.

The Israeli Nature and Parks authority took upon itself the task of transforming Wadi Hilweh from 'an intolerable illegal dwelling of thousands [of Palestinians]' into a tourist-accessible Jewish attraction,[3] presenting the doctrine of the prominent late architect Arieh Sharon as its guiding principle:

> The site of the City of David … is of great archaeological importance. A nondescript neighbourhood has recently sprung up here, with many ugly buildings.… Since the resettlement of hundreds of families is an extremely expensive task, the liquidation of this neighbourhood should be thought of

in terms of a long-range policy; no new building should be permitted, plots should be gradually purchased and families relocated in new areas.

(Sharon *et al.*, 1973, p. 204)

Indeed, 40 years later, Sharon's plan to liquidate the existing Palestinian presence has been partially implemented: some Palestinian homes were demolished and others were purchased or expropriated for the benefit of Jewish-Israeli settlers, while the neighbourhood was slowly transformed into a national and archaeological attraction aimed at the consumption of tourists and the enlargement of the Jewish urban space adjacent to the Western Wall. I posit that these steps, as part of a state-led project, were aided and enabled by a large-scale security intervention in the area of Silwan, which can be defined by the prominent performances of 'showing presence' and the practice of maintaining deliberate friction by the security actors on site. In tracing the state effects which re-configure the space, materiality and imagery of Wadi Hilweh, we encounter a wide array of different security actors working within and at the margins of the state in close cooperation.

Security for the Jewish-Israeli settlers at the City of David site, as in other Jewish-Israeli settlement compounds in East Jerusalem, is provided by both public and private security agents. The Israeli Police and the Israeli Border Police corps are nominally in charge of the security of Palestinian residents and Jewish-Israeli settlers alike, while a large number of private security guards, employed by a private security company and financed by the Israeli Ministry of Housing, are in charge of the personal security of the settlers, their guests and

Figure 6.1 Private armed escort at the entrance to the City of David National Park.

Raising the flag 103

property. The private security guards are positioned 24/7 at the entrance of or in a watchtower above each of the settlement compounds – private residences, offices and the site of the archaeological site's visitors centre. Security cameras were installed at every compound, remotely controlled to zoom in on events happening both within the settlement compounds, in public areas and at the nearby Palestinian homes (see Figure 6.1).

For Hussam, the continuous presence of security agents in his neighbourhood marks a tremendous change from the former days of little police activity, patrols or interest. Inside the small grocery shop, he enjoys talking at length about the neighbourhood's past as well as the Jewish-Israeli religious settlers who moved in accompanied by security guards and policemen. Waving his hands around in a theatrical fashion, Hussam recalled:

> Everything that used to be has by now changed.... The private security guards are everywhere in our neighbourhood, on our roads. In the mornings we have to wait for an hour in traffic when they block the roads and pick up the settlers' children for school; if another car blocks them they shout using megaphones, waking up the entire neighbourhood. I used to be able to sit down in the evening in one of the yards, share a meal or a chat. Now the settlers would call the police, which will arrive in a minute together with the Magav [border police], and threaten us to go back inside our home.

The continuous presence of security agents in and near the City of David National Park plays an important role in the transformation of the neighbourhood from a quiet Palestinian locale into a series of regimented securitized spaces of exclusion. In these, an effective limitation of rights takes place as a result of policing practices at the legal margins (Basaran, 2008). Hussam described how public and private security agents dominate – or even monopolize – public spaces through the mundane practices of unequal mobility. Jewish-Israeli settlers are provided free transport services by the private security guards, which are constantly on stand-by to drive them and their children to West Jerusalem, the Old City or other settlement compounds. A Russian-born Israeli former security guard in his early 30s, who later became a software engineer, recalled in an interview that 'we [private security guards in Silwan] operated like a taxi station. All day and all night we had to be prepared in each sector with two transit vans, in case the settlers wanted to go somewhere'.

Instead of the secured movement experienced by the settlers, Palestinian residents are subjected to the difficulties associated with impeded mobility and a continuous sense of uncertainty and insecurity. The movement of Palestinian residents and vehicles is subjected to the whims of policemen and private security guards, who limit their movement with ad-hoc checkpoints or by causing long traffic jams while servicing the Jewish-Israeli settlers. The impact of this differentiation may not be measured only in the quantitative terms of lost working hours or the length of necessary detours, but rather in the longue durée effects of marginalization and alienation of Palestinian residents from their own

104 *Lior Volinz*

homes. Hussam referred to the shifting perceptions of Palestinian children, who encounter the Israeli security guards on a daily basis from a young age:

> Try and think about what the presence of all these security guards is doing to our neighbourhood. For example, one of the Palestinian kids here, he doesn't have much at home; he sees one of the settlers' boys walking around the street with two armed bodyguards, one in the front the other in the back. He asks himself: '*Who is this kid?*', '*Why is he so important?*', and then he slowly figures out that it's no longer his home, his neighbourhood, but rather that of the boys with the security guards.

The conspicuous activities of private security guards in and around the City of David National Park are aimed at 'showing presence' – an aggressive performance aimed at simultaneously reassuring some and deterring others (Grassiani, 2013; Grassiani and Volinz, 2016). The private security guards provide security in a differential manner – they divide the population into those who are in need of protection and those who are considered a threat. They reassure the first about their safety in hostile territory, while intimidating the latter into compliance. This might seem a simple statement regarding the roles enacted by a private security company towards a paying customer; yet in this case, the paying customer is the state itself. The employment, deployment and tactics of private security guards at the City of David National Park are coordinated and financed by the Israeli Ministry of Housing and the Israeli Police. Their undertakings are subject to the terms of a lengthy public tender, which determines nearly every aspect of the private security operations, from their type of ammunition, to obligations towards the settlers, even to the appropriate air conditioning installation in their watchtowers.

The outsourced private security provision is understood by both the settlers and the private security guards themselves as a fulfilment of the state's obligation to protect its citizens. While the security company remains a private commercial enterprise, it underwent reconfiguration as part and parcel of the larger Israeli public–private security array in East Jerusalem. When a private security guard conducts patrols, provides armed escorts or handles traffic on the road, the thin line separating him from a public security agent, such as a policeman, becomes increasingly blurred. Both public and private security agents are armed with similar weapons, use a common police radio for communication, conduct patrols and initialize interventions when the need arises. The security practices employed by the private guards become inseparable from the larger state-led project of transforming Wadi Hilweh from a Palestinian urban dwelling into a Jewish-themed attraction. By 'showing presence' in and around the City of David National Park, the private security guards reinforce the visibility and accessibility of the settlers' enterprise to visiting outsiders, while marginalizing and ultimately minimalizing the presence of the local residents of the neighbourhood. Their mundane work practices co-compose state effects: not Mitchell's (1999) state of public structures and individual agency or the deterritorialized

Raising the flag 105

state of Trouillot, Hann and Krti (2001), but rather the state effects of an increasingly hybrid public–private national order.

For many Palestinian residents, the different Israeli public and private security agents in Wadi Hilweh are largely indistinguishable from one another; for others, the different legal capacities and obligations of security actors provide either an opportunity or an obstacle to challenge their actions. When another white armoured van used by the security guards passed by, Hussam remarked on the negative role of private security guards in the neighbourhood:

> They might behave like they're policemen but we know that they're never impartial – they take the settlers' side on every occasion. Once, down here [pointing at another house down the road] a Palestinian resident was having an argument with a settler over a parking spot. The private security guards rushed over and dispersed the Palestinian and his family by shooting in the air – when the police drove over they were told by the security guards that 'it's all been taken care of'.

Wadi Hilweh is a small and dense neighbourhood, with tensions fuelled by the settlers' national park enterprise contributing to violent confrontations between settlers, security personnel and the local Palestinian residents in and around the neighbourhood. These range from fist fights to stone throwing, Molotov cocktail attacks and the occasional shoot-out. In 2010 Wadi Hilweh made headlines when a 32-year-old Palestinian resident named Samer Sarhan was killed by a private security guard near the City of David National Park. Yet it is the day-to-day friction and violent encounters between residents and security personnel, such as the parking incident just described, in which the mundane practices of the private security guards come to the fore. The nuanced interplay between public and private security provision in this case is presented as significant to all the actors involved: the private security guards, the Israeli policemen, the Jewish-Israeli settlers and the Palestinian residents.

The private security guards are somewhat aware of their limited legal authority and capacity: every security guard working in the East Jerusalem settlement project undergoes compulsory legal training followed by an elementary examination. Intervening in a non-physical quarrel between neighbours in a public space by discharging an automatic weapon is outside their jurisdiction. By highlighting their partnership with the policemen ('it's been taken care of'), they were able to evade scrutiny while catering to the interests of the settlers under their protection. The policemen, who would normally attempt to settle the dispute and question both sides involved, preferred instead to delegate this role to the private security guards. The unauthorized usage of a firearm by a person considered a fellow security agent was not deemed worthwhile to investigate further.

The Jewish-Israeli settlers benefited from an advantage over their neighbours in the form of a personal security guard provided by the state. Nearly all of the private security guards I've interviewed complained of the settlers' tendency to exacerbate conflicts with the local Palestinian residents while expecting the security guards to intervene on their behalf. Since the CCTV cameras situated on almost every corner are operated exclusively by the private security company, any visual evidence of Palestinian violence is quickly sent to the police for further prosecution. Evidence of Jewish-settlers' violence (and that of the security guards themselves), on the other hand, is often reviewed 'in-house' and not sent to the police even when specific requests from the Palestinian residents are made. For the Jewish-Israeli settlers, this state of affairs lends a certain impunity to their actions in and around the City of David National Park, one which might be diminished by the presence of regular police forces (see Figure 6.2).

Among the Palestinian residents of Wadi Hilweh there is broad agreement that despite the violence inflicted by the regular police forces and the much-despised border police, communicating with public security agents is preferable to dealing with the private security guards.[4] With the regular policemen one might plead or negotiate; with the private security guards there is little possibility of reaching a compromise or invoking legal rights and obligations. Hussam lamented that:

> Unlike the border policemen, who are usually wearing an identifying tag on their shirts, we have no clue who the private security guards are – and they never give us their names if asked. So no matter what they do, we can't complain ... they're a group of their own, above the law.

Figure 6.2 Guardhouse above a Jewish-Israeli settlement compound in Silwan.

In 2011, residents of Silwan together with the Association for Civil Rights in Israel filed a legal appeal against the procurement and deployment of private security guards in and around Jewish-Israeli settlers' compounds in East Jerusalem. Voicing concerns similar to the ones outlined above, the appeal emphasized previous Israeli governmental unfulfilled decisions to return the security provision at Silwan's settlement compounds back to the police authority. The Israeli High Court of Justice rejected the appeal in 2014, accepting the state's position that the private security guards do not engage in 'policing', but rather in permitted personal protection services (ACRI, 2014).

I suggest that the impetus to hire private security guards to protect the Jewish-Israeli settlers at the City of David National Park is a deliberate political consideration. Financially, outsourcing the security provision at the site instead of using border police conscripts makes little sense: an estimated 30,000 NIS (~€7000) are spent annually per Jewish-Israeli settler for the private security guards protecting those residing in the East Jerusalem settlement compounds, including the City of David (Haaretz, 2014). Unlike with public security providers, private security companies allow the Israeli authorities the legal and operational flexibility needed to provide an ostensible differential security provision which favours one group of residents over the other. In the Occupied West Bank, policymakers are not faced with such a dilemma, since West Bank Palestinians are subjected to military law, and the army is regularly deployed to suppress any dissent. In East Jerusalem, which the Israeli government annexed and imposed its laws upon, the Israeli army is not directly engaging Palestinian Jerusalemites. Private security provision enables the state to give precedence to the security and safety of the Jewish-Israeli settlers over that of the local residents – a discrimination on ethnic and national lines which still conforms to the Israeli legislation and the illusion of a united Jerusalem.

Yet what do these practices tell us about how the state is crafted? Where is the state going when the provision of security at national parks is outsourced to a for-profit actor? I argue that the private security guards' practices at the City of David National Park co-constitute state effects: they contribute to the assertion of sovereignty over the occupied territory in a manner which public security actors are unwilling or unable to manifest. The state-led project of transforming the Palestinian neighbourhoods in the vicinity of Jerusalem's Old City into a Jewish-dominant attraction and residential space includes public and private security actors alike. The private security agents involved are an extension of the public security providers – the former complement the latter in the murky waters of legal and operational liminality enshrouding the displacement of Palestinian residents in the heart of Jerusalem, one of the world's holiest cities.

The state is crafted in and around the City of David National Park through the physical takeover of space, through the materialities and visualities of flags, Hebrew-language signs and gated spaces, which are designed for consumption by foreign visitors and are devoid of the threatening presence of local residents. Yet it is through a conspicuous public and private security provision that the state is able to assert its sovereignty and territorially encompass Wadi Hilweh as

108   *Lior Volinz*

part of a veneer of a united Jerusalem. Rather than engendering a competition over legitimacy and sovereignty between public and private security providers, the private security guards in Wadi Hilweh are becoming intermeshed with the state-led project. Their practices are aimed at performing the state – a performance of 'showing presence' which asserts sovereignty, reassures some residents and intimidates others. Private security agents figuratively and literally raise the flag of the state in an occupied territory, under governmental orders yet without the legal restrictions, accountability or the political burden involved in deploying soldiers or regular policemen.

Policing at the edge of the state: security encounters and deliberate friction

Sometimes, the margins of the state may be located in close proximity to its core. The rolling hills south of Jerusalem's Old City offer a panoramic view of the Haram al-Sharif or Temple Mount, the golden Dome of the Rock glistening in plain view from the thousands of houses built on the steep slopes. Silwan, Jabel Mukaber, Abu Tor and Ras al-Amud are some of the Palestinian neighbourhoods that are located near the contested holy sites, yet enjoy little in the way of proper urban planning or social, educational or infrastructural investments by the Israeli municipal or state authorities. Those locales do, however, warrant close attention by the authorities in one respect: a continuous project of replacing Palestinian inhabitants with Jewish-Israeli settlers is going on in each of these neighbourhoods, a process which is causing a 'mixture of exclusion, neighbourhood abandonment and warehousing of Palestinian residents' (Dumper and Pullan, 2010). This area, under continuous occupation and contestation, is at the core of the State of Israel and at the same time at its far frontiers. That might be a combustible blend – as Mbembe and Meintjes (2003, p. 24) remind us, 'Frontiers are "zones" … where the violence of the state of exception is deemed to operate in the service of "civilization"'.

What practices and performances are pursued in the effort to transform, 'civilize' or 'Judaize' a space? Cook and Whowell (2011) suggest that the police undertake performances crafted to deter illegal behaviour through an interplay of visible and invisible embodied performances. I continue to inquire into how the residents of these neighbourhoods understand and explain these performances, enacted as part of an increased police presence throughout the neighbourhoods. The following section will look at the policing strategies and performances employed by public security actors in Silwan, particularly in and around Wadi Hilweh/City of David National Park.

To illustrate the encounters between police agents and Palestinian residents, I begin with a short ethnographic description of an incident in May 2015 in the Old City's Dung Gate, situated at the edge of the City of David National Park. The gate, built in the sixteenth century, allows for the movement of people and vehicles into the Jewish quarter; a few paces away from the Western Wall, Jewish-Israeli and international visitors come by foot or by bus on their way to

Raising the flag 109

worship at the holy site. Palestinian residents of Silwan have used the gate for centuries to enter the Old City, including on their journey to pray on the Haram al-Sharif or Temple mount. Nowadays, however, severe limitations imposed by Israeli policemen prevent many Palestinians from travelling freely through the Dung Gate and into the Jewish quarter; instead, many residents are forced to take a longer route, entering through a different gate to avoid tense encounters with Israeli security forces.

On a spring day I was sitting by the Dung Gate with Isaam, an informant residing in Silwan, a burly man in his 40s who preferred to talk about football, or his children, rather than politics. At the Dung Gate three armed border policemen were watching everyone entering the Old City. They have a tiny guardhouse of their own, with an Israeli flag on top, but usually they stand outside in the open air (see Figure 6.3). Above the gate three CCTV cameras record any entry to and exit from the Old City; they are part of a police initiative named 'Mabat 2000' which captures video streams from security cameras throughout the Old City, to be observed in a central command room. Hundreds of Jewish-Israeli visitors and international tourists are going back and forth, many heading onto one of the tourist buses to continue their journey. Isaam used to work in one of the Palestinian souvenir shops by the gate; he knows the names of most of the Israeli policemen and private security guards working in the area, so occasionally he waves at one of the squad cars passing. I first notice a Palestinian man approaching the gate when one border policeman shouts to his partner: 'Get over here, fast!' The urgent call was the result of this single Palestinian man trying to enter the Old City. The man was asked to hand over his ID, which he dutifully did.

Figure 6.3 The Old City's Dung Gate.

110 *Lior Volinz*

Upon seeing the green colour of the man's ID, which revealed that he was a West Bank resident, the policeman called over his colleague. Together they began questioning the man in Hebrew and inspecting his possessions. Where are you from? Since when do you live in Silwan? Why do you want to go to the Jewish quarter?

Witnessing the policeman patting down the man, Isaam made a move to intervene: 'If he has a permit, why don't you let him go? ... Of course he wants to enter the gate, it's the quickest way to the Old City'. To no avail; the policeman called for backup to detain the man and send him for questioning at the central police station. Isaam had just enough time to bring the detainee a cup of tea and assure him that chances were high he'd be released that day and spend the night back home with his Jerusalemite family. Isaam came back deflated:

> Look how well they take care of the settlers and of the tourists. They're free to go where they want. But for us [Silwan residents] the police and Magav [border police] usually represent nothing but checkpoints, raids, humiliation and fear of leaving your neighbourhood.

Isaam points out the difference between the police obligation to protect all residents equally, and the practices employed by policemen in East Jerusalem, which differentiate between the Palestinian and Jewish residents. Aharon Franko, the former head of the Jerusalem district police, argued in a Knesset session that 'I treat all residents equally ... I should provide equal protection for a Jew who resides in Sheiqh' Jarrah or a Palestinian in East Jerusalem. That's the job we were given' (Knesset Internal Affairs Committee, 2010). Yet the policing practices employed at the Dung Gate, and at national parks in East Jerusalem in general, elucidate a picture of unofficial ethnic profiling. These include ad-hoc checkpoints, established in certain locales with the aim of limiting and scrutinizing Palestinian movement, while enabling unimpeded mobility by Jewish-Israeli citizens and international tourists. The security encounters at these sites, ordinary as they might be, are paramount to the state effects they compose, namely the difference between the formal obligation to equal protection and the differentially applied performative practices employed by the policemen. I argue that this gap, applied in practice and largely unbound by legal limitations, forms a significant state effect with which Israel is able to continue its occupation of East Jerusalem, while simultaneously maintaining the veneer of a united city under one law. The city's national parks, and the Wadi Hilweh/City of David site in particular, provide a relevant case study of how security is performed at the margins of the state, contributing at the same time to the assertion of the state's (unequal or graduated) sovereignty over an occupied territory, the displacement of some residents and the unimpeded mobility of others.

The policing of the dense Palestinian neighbourhoods of East Jerusalem is done in the narrow lanes and alleys of the sprawling urban space; any police and border police presence necessitates a high level of friction with the local residents. Yet at the City of David National Park and the surrounding Palestinian

Raising the flag 111

residential space, Israeli security agents engage in practices aimed at producing deliberate friction with the Palestinian residents. Ahmed, a Palestinian resident of Wadi Hilweh, talked to me at length about his experiences residing near an Israeli-Jewish settlement compound. He works hard and provides well for his family; he has two daughters and a son, all of school age. His concern lies mostly with the impact of the presence of different Israeli security agents on his children. He says that heavily armed border policemen deliberately wait outside the local schools during the morning and afternoon hours, precisely at the time of the pupils' arrival and departure. 'It's done on purpose – they want to provoke the pupils to make some trouble and get them into a fight', he says:

> Maybe you see the border policemen and you think they're there to protect the school, but they're in fact ordered to wait there till a pupil hurls an insult or a stone, and then they take out their tear gas grenades and rubber bullets and then everything explodes,

he says, while mimicking an explosion with his hands.

Ahmed and other Palestinian residents bemoan policing practices, which engender deliberate friction between policemen and residents; assuming that violence is inevitable, policemen provoke violent encounters in predetermined spaces and moments rather than face unexpected bursts of confrontations with angry youth. Violence can thus be channelled – the police take the initiative by provoking violence which pre-empts possible surprises that may harm the security, accessibility or property of the nearby national park. This practice goes beyond merely enhancing police presence in the streets and diverges from both the harsh 'broken window' policing which emphasizes zero tolerance to minor forms of disorder (Mitchell, 2010) and the performance of 'showing presence' in contested sites. Instead, Israeli border policemen engage in a practice which can be understood as both preventative and provocative: violent encounters are sought rather than averted, while the spaces frequented by tourists and Israeli-Jewish visitors remain devoid of signs of violent resistance. These practices unequally distribute the burden of violence and repression associated with the dispossession and displacement of residents, shifting it away from the touted national parks and the Old City and towards the core of the Palestinian neighbourhoods. Ahmed commented on the transformation of Wadi Hilweh as a whole and his personal life in particular:

> It's the constant presence of border-police personnel which has turned the entire neighbourhood upside down ... I no longer allow my daughter to go to the school, the shop or her friends on her own, our roads are left closed because of the whim of a bunch of kids in uniform and I can't sit on my porch without the sneaky feeling that somebody is watching.... What was once a calm neighbourhood is now a battlefield.

Conclusion

Inquiring into the characteristics of the state can be a daunting task: the state might be simultaneously absent and excessively present – its materialities and visualities in East Jerusalem consisted of both perilous roads and shiny tourist reception centres, both lawless streets and the omnipresence of security agents. I elected to focus on the mundane practices of security in a national park in East Jerusalem with the aim of turning our attention to the state effects with which the state is crafted. The state effects asserting Israeli sovereignty in East Jerusalem are differentiated, modular and legally precarious. Outsourcing the national park security provision allows state authorities to distance themselves from discriminatory or violent practices, while contributing to the private agents' flexibility and unaccountability. Security can thus be performed in a manner customized to different audiences: Jewish-Israeli settlers, Palestinian residents, and domestic and international visitors.

The public and private cooperation in the security provision at the City of David National Park brings us back to the suggestion of Trouillot, Hann and Krti (2001) that state effects are increasingly found outside the national state, with global and local actors partaking in the performance of the state and the (re)production of its materialities, visualities and spatial presence. They posit that state effects, even when pursued by private actors, never entirely bypass the national order. Indeed, in the City of David National Park it seemed that private security provision and the Jewish-Israeli settler organizations were in continuous gravitation towards the state: sometimes serving as a proxy to state actors while at other times deliberately distancing themselves from the authority and obligations of the state. Rather than simply mimicking state actors, private security guards are able to pursue policies that public security agents are reluctant or unable to do. In an awkward conflation, the state effects produced by private actors can surpass those of public agents – they can 'show presence' better and assert the state's sovereignty in hostile territory with little to no resistance. Unbound by much of the legal and political considerations limiting the police, private security guards represent a state-led project in its distilled form of security to some and displacement for others. Flying not one but 100 Israeli flags, both literally and figuratively, private security guards perform the state while engaging in mundane security practices – thus becoming an integral part of the Israeli occupation regime in East Jerusalem.

The challenges faced by public security agents in East Jerusalem prompt the adoption of specific practices and materialities developed with attention to the legal and political considerations of East Jerusalem in mind. These practices, such as the ones employed by policemen at the City of David National Park, reflect the state-led project of growing Jewish-Israeli presence in Palestinian neighbourhoods in and around the Old City. In this chapter I aimed to show how the manoeuvres of policemen on the ground, including impeding residents' mobility and seeking deliberate friction, reinforced the differential provision of security in East Jerusalem, which favours the security of Jewish-Israeli settlers

Raising the flag 113

over that of the Palestinian residents. I proposed that this gap of (in)security forms a significant state effect with which graduated sovereignty is extended into the occupied neighbourhoods of East Jerusalem.

The City of David National Park, situated in the Palestinian neighbourhood of Wadi Hilweh, is just one example of a site where unequal provision of security leads to the transformation of residential space and differential application of disciplinary violence. While national parks are often considered neutral spaces of conformity, in this chapter I aimed to show how a 'green' area of conservation and heritage can simultaneously be located at the margins of the state, the contours of its public–private security provision crafted and extended so as to implement a state-led project. By drawing attention to the practices of security actors at a national park, the plurality of the state effects aimed at asserting sovereignty in an occupied territory come to the fore. Located within and outside of the formal state, the state effects of public and private security providers reconfigure the frontiers of the state and the contours of its sovereignty.

Notes

1 East Jerusalem was annexed de-facto by Israel in June 1967, when the municipal line was re-drawn; in 1980 the annexation of East Jerusalem was completed de-jure following the passing of the *Jerusalem Basic Law* in the Israeli Knesset.
2 See also Ir Amim (2012).
3 See Nature and Parks Authority (2009).
4 On the comparison of the violent measures used by public and private security agents in Silwan see: ACRI – The Association for Civil Rights in Israel (2009).

References

Abrams, P., 1988. Notes on the difficulty of studying the state (1977). *Journal of Historical Sociology*, 1(1), pp. 58–89.
ACRI – The Association for Civil Rights in Israel, 2009. *Unsafe space: the Israeli authorities' failure to protect human rights amid settlements in East Jerusalem* [online]. Available at: www.acri.org.il/pdf/unsafe-space-en.pdf [accessed July 2015].
ACRI – The Association for Civil Rights in Israel, 2014. *Appeal against the operation of private security guards in East Jerusalem; File Bagatz 8001/11* [online]. Available at: www.acri.org.il/he/24437 [Hebrew] [accessed July 2015].
Basaran, T., 2008. Security, law, borders: spaces of exclusion. *International Political Sociology*, 2(4), pp. 339–354.
Cook, I.R. and Whowell, M., 2011. Visibility and the policing of public space. *Geography Compass*, 5(8), pp. 610–622.
Dumper, M., 2013. Policing divided cities: stabilization and law enforcement in Palestinian east Jerusalem. *International Affairs*, 89(5), pp. 1247–1264.
Dumper, M. and Pullan, W., 2010. *Jerusalem: the cost of failure*. London: Chatham House/Royal Institute of International Affairs.
Giddens, A., 1979. *Central problems in social theory: action, structure, and contradiction in social analysis* (vol. 241). Berkeley, CA: University of California Press.
Goldstein, D.M., 2015. Color-coded sovereignty and the men in black: private security in a Bolivian marketplace. *Conflict and Society: Advances in Research*, 1(1), pp. 182–196.

114 *Lior Volinz*

Grassiani, E., 2013. *Soldiering under occupation: processes of numbing among Israeli soldiers in the Al-Aqsa intifada.* New York: Berghahn Books.

Grassiani, E. and Volinz, L., 2016. Intimidation, reassurance and invisibility: Israeli security agents in the Old City of Jerusalem. *Focaal,* 75, pp. 14–30.

Greenberg, R., 2009. Towards an inclusive archaeology in Jerusalem: the case of Silwan/ the City of David. *Public Archaeology,* 8(1), pp. 35–50.

Haaretz, 2014. Hasson Nir: the cost of providing security to a Jewish resident in East Jerusalem has surpassed 30,000 NIS this year. *Haartez* [online]. Available at: www. haaretz.co.il/.premium-1.2492751 [Hebrew] [accessed July 2015].

Hansen, T.B., 2006. Performers of sovereignty on the privatization of security in urban South Africa. *Critique of Anthropology,* 26(3), pp. 279–295.

Havkin, S., 2014. *The privatization of the checkpoints in the West Bank and the Gaza strip: policy paper.* Jerusalem: Van Leer Institute.

Ir Amim, 2012. *Report: the giant's garden* [pdf]. Available at: www.ir-amim.org.il/sites/ default/files/el%20bustan%20HEB.pdf [Hebrew] [accessed 10 July 2015].

Khamisi, R., 2015. Conference notes. In: JIIS. *Between East and West: equality and inequality in Jerusalem.* Jerusalem, 6 July 2015.

Knesset Internal Affairs Committee, 2010. *Protocol dated 22 December 2010* [Hebrew]. Available at: www.knesset.gov.il/protocols/data/rtf/pnim/2010-12-22.rtf [accessed July 2015].

Konopinski, N., 2009. *Ordinary security: an ethnography of security practices and perspectives in Tel Aviv.* Edinburgh: University of Edinburgh.

Loader, I., 1999. Consumer culture and the commodification of policing and security. *Sociology,* 33(2), pp. 373–392.

Mbembe, J. and Meintjes, L., 2003. Necropolitics. *Public Culture,* 15(1), pp. 11–40.

Mitchell, K., 2010. Ungoverned space: global security and the geopolitics of broken windows. *Political Geography,* 29(5), pp. 289–297.

Mitchell, T., 1999. Society, economy, and the state effect. In: G. Steinmetz, ed., *State/ culture: state-formation after the cultural turn.* Ithaca, NY: Cornell University Press.

Nature and Parks Authority, 2009. *Jerusalem Walls National Park, planning principles and programs status* [online]. Available at: www.parks.org.il/ParksAndReserves/city-ofDavidJerusalemWalls/Pages/default.aspx [Hebrew] [accessed July 2015].

Ong, A., 2000. Graduated sovereignty in south-east Asia. *Theory, Culture & Society,* 17(4), pp. 55–75.

Ortner, S.B., 2006. Introduction: updating practice theory. *Anthropology and social theory: culture, power, and the acting subject.* Durham, NC and London: Duke University Press.

Pullan, W. and Gwiazda, M., 2009. City of David: urban design and frontier heritage. *Jerusalem Quarterly,* 39, pp. 29–38.

Pullan, W., Misselwitz, P., Nasrallah, R. and Yacobi, H., 2007. Jerusalem's road 1: an inner city frontier? *City,* 11(2), pp. 176–198.

Russell, B., 2012. *Social research methods: qualitative and quantitative approaches.* London: Sage.

Sharon, A., Brutzkus, D.A., Mordohovich, H. and Sharon, E., 1973. *Planning Jerusalem: the old city and its environs.* Jerusalem: Weidenfeld and Nicolson.

Stepputat, F., 2015. Formations of sovereignty at the frontier of the modern state. *Conflict and Society: Advances in Research,* 1(1), pp. 129–143.

Trouillot, M., Hann, C. and Krti, L., 2001. The anthropology of the state in the age of globalization 1: close encounters of the deceptive kind. *Current Anthropology,* 42(1), pp. 125–138.

Part III

Democratic control and ethical implications

7 Evaluation and effectiveness of counter-terrorism

Fiona de Londras

Introduction

In the past decade and a half there has been an enormous expansion of counter-terrorism laws and policies at national, regional and international levels. Spurred on by the events of 9/11 and, later, the phenomena of the so-called Islamic state and of 'foreign terrorist fighters', states and international institutions have introduced laws and policies that encroach greatly on fundamental freedoms and human rights, and the international conception of the 'rule of law' has been 'securitized' to a striking degree so that it now increasingly suggests 'strong' institutions capable of effective coercion rather than necessarily limited, transparent and rights-bound institutions, answerable to 'the People'. Domestic and international counter-terrorism measures include provisions to permit, require and fund technologically innovative approaches to counter-terrorism. Thus, surveillance, smart borders, data collection and sharing, passenger name record exchange and so on feature heavily in the highly technologized arena of contemporary counter-terrorism where the production, retention, processing and deployment of data have taken centre stage. While these measures raise particular questions flowing from the technologies applied, this chapter takes a step back from the specifics of technological innovation in security to address a matter of structural, ethical and deliberative concern across the field of security: effectiveness.

In the field of counter-terrorism, evaluation of whether counter-terrorist measures are actually effective is worryingly inadequate or, sometimes, simply non-existent. Given the implications of expansive counter-terrorism for human rights, democracy and the Rule of Law, I will argue that the evaluation of effectiveness is fundamental in maintaining the legitimacy of the counter-terrorist state and supra-state. Having done that, I will explore what the notion of 'effectiveness' means in this context, identifying both meta- and specific objectives as critical sites of analysis. Based on this, the chapter will argue for the implementation of critical, reflexive and comprehensive *ex post facto* effectiveness evaluation of counter-terrorist measures, going well beyond a mere analysis of 'legality' per se. Where done properly, such evaluation should enhance legitimacy, not least by identifying areas where the infringement of personal liberty resulting from a

118   *Fiona de Londras*

counter-terrorism measure is disproportionate to its apparent effectiveness in enhancing security.

Framing context

It goes without saying that terrorism and counter-terrorism did not begin on 11 September 2001. For many countries, violence labelled as 'terrorist' had been a constant reality for decades. For others, such violence was more sporadic, but no less serious. Some, although not many, states had bodies of law known as 'anti-terrorism law' or 'counter-terrorism' law. Most others dealt with behaviours now commonly termed 'terrorist' through the ordinary criminal law. Thus, laws and policies with implications for rights, devised and executed pursuant to a security rationale, are nothing new at the domestic level.

It is also not the case that transnationalism in terrorism is an entirely new phenomenon. Organizations deemed 'terrorist' had, in some cases, well-established patterns of cross-border cooperation, training and arms trading or supply that stretched back many years before the attacks on the Pentagon and the World Trade Centre. Neither was ostentatiousness in methods of terrorist attacks unknown. Shopping centre bombings, suicide bombings, assassinations, hijacking and even bombing civilian aircraft were all known to us by September 2001.

Yet, for all of that, the attacks of 9/11 – as they have become known – did change the world of counter-terrorism in ways that can only be hinted at in this chapter, but which fundamentally shape the context in which we must think about the questions of justification for, effectiveness of and impacts of counter-terrorism measures and operations, including technological innovations in security and counter-terrorism. For our purposes, four examples of this change are germane.

First, we saw the emergence of a transnational counter-terrorism hegemon in the shape of the United States and the United Kingdom combined. This hegemon – understood in Gramscian terms as a 'ruling class' that 'maintain[s] their dominance by securing the "spontaneous consent" of subordinate groups … through the negotiated construction of a political and ideological consensus which incorporates both dominant and dominated groups' (Strinati, 1995, p. 165) – embarked on a concerted effort to shift prevailing legal attitudes in domestic and international law in respect of what is, and what is not, permitted in the name of inter/national security. These states did not take precisely the same approach to this effort – I have previously said that the United States mounted an 'external challenge' to human rights law, disputing its very applicability to the 'War on Terror', while the United Kingdom's was an 'internal challenge' aimed at recalibrating downwards the meaning and content of key rights (de Londras, 2011) – but on the whole, a similar commitment to transforming the legal and political landscape is discernible. Both states were determined to ensure that international law permitted – or could be interpreted as permitting – what they considered to be 'necessary' to 'counter terrorism'. This included enhanced interrogation (rhetorically, although not substantively, differentiated from torture), deportation,

Evaluation of counter-terrorism 119

trial without jury, inequality of arms within the criminal justice system, targeted killing, drone warfare outside of the traditionally defined 'theatre of war', mass surveillance and data retention. In respect of such measures, the political mantra often appeared to be 'it is legal, and if it is not we will make it so'; a position that displays a somewhat confounding commitment to the concept of legality positivistically understood, on the one hand, and rejection of the autonomy and limiting force of law purposively understood, on the other.

While the United States and United Kingdom have not succeeded in shifting the contours of international law, including international human rights law, as substantially as they appear to have desired, they have nevertheless achieved such downward calibration that 'gisting' (*A & Others* v. *United Kingdom*, European Court of Human Rights, 2009), protracted detention without charge (*A & Others* v. *United Kingdom*, European Court of Human Rights, 2009), control orders and similar mechanisms of what Zedner calls 'pre-punishment' (Zedner, 2007), and deportation with assurances are now all stamped 'human rights compliant' – sometimes even considered human rights victories – when they would have been simply unthinkable 20 years ago (de Londras, 2014).

The second trend of note is the internationalization of counter-terrorism law making. Prior to 11 September 2001, the so-called 'international community' had taken some notice of terrorism, but in a fragmented and ad hoc manner. Efforts to have more comprehensive international law on counter-terrorism had long been frustrated by the dynamics and debates of (post-)colonialism, resistance, assumed legitimacy of state force and the Israel–Palestine conflict (Grozdanova, 2014). Thus, while more than a dozen international conventions had a counter-terrorism element, there was (and remains) no comprehensive, legally binding definition of terrorism in international law (Grozdanova, 2014). Prior to 9/11 this definitional gap and the underlying political and ideological definitions it exposed, together with states' tight hold on security as a sovereign concern, had the effect of stymying more unified action on counter-terrorism. After the attacks of 9/11, however, the reluctance to act en masse as an 'international community' quickly fell away.

At both international and regional levels, counter-terrorism became an area of concerted action. The first hints that this would be so came with the extraordinary Resolution 1373 from the UN Security Council on 28 September 2001, the invocation of Article 5 of the Washington Treaty by NATO on 12 September (committing members of NATO to protect each other under the principle of collective defense) and the release of the EU's agreed Action Plan to Counter Terrorism on 21 September (outlining a comprehensive approach to counter-terrorism to be pursued at the EU level). The speed of these developments – highly unusual in international affairs – was matched by the expanse of the content and implications of these actions. This is well illustrated by the Security Council Resolution 1373 itself. This Resolution directed all member states of the United Nations to introduce laws preventing, suppressing and criminalizing activities relating to terrorist fundraising (Operative Paragraph 1(a), (b), (c), SC Resolution 1373 (2001)), freeze funds and assets of those involved in or associated with terrorism (Operative Paragraph 1(d), SC Resolution 1373 (2001)), and prohibit material support for terrorism (Operative Paragraph 1(e), SC Resolution 1373 (2001)). In addition, states were directed to refrain from supporting terrorist activity, and to '[t]ake the necessary steps to prevent the commission of terrorist acts' including through providing information to other states, providing assistance to other states in investigating and prosecuting terrorist financing or support, preventing the movement of terrorists through their borders, and refusing safe haven to terrorist actors and activities (Operative Paragraph 2, SC Resolution 1373 (2001)). States were 'called upon' to improve mechanisms of exchanging operational information on terrorism and terrorist activities, and broadly to enhance their cooperation in the field of counter-terrorism (Operative Paragraph 2, SC Resolution 1373 (2001)). The Resolution went on to establish the Counter-Terrorism Committee with broad coordinating and capacity-enhancing functions, as well as functions relating to the implementation of counter-terrorist sanctions (Operative Paragraph 6, SC Resolution 1373 (2001)). As I have written elsewhere:

> Resolution 1373 set the ground conditions for a significant internationalisation of counter-terrorism, with the Security Council effectively acting as a proxy legislator for all member states as well as establishing counter-terrorist cooperation as an international good, if not an expectation of membership of the international community of states committed to the maintenance of peace and security.
>
> (de Londras, 2017)

One of the most notable – and debated – elements of this Resolution (and of the Foreign Fighters Resolution that followed in September 2014 (Security Council Resolution 2178 (2014))) is that it effectively required domestic parliaments to pass certain criminal laws if they did not already exist on the statute book. As these Resolutions are passed under Chapter VII of the UN Charter they are legally binding for all member states. This brings us to the third trend of relevance here: the expansion of domestic counter-terrorism law in a democratically questionable manner.

It is not only Chapter VII Resolutions that raise this concern: so too do Framework Decisions and Directives at EU level, and indeed bi- and multilateral treaty and development tie-ins requiring states to take certain approaches to the legal regulation of (counter-)terrorism, where those treaties are 'negotiated' in circumstances of economic or other inequality, thereby belying the myth of state equality in international law. In other words, international forces are now substantially shaping counter-terrorism: an area previously largely left to domestic politics and policy. Of course, this is not unique to counter-terrorism: it happens in many areas of transnational activity and regulation. Given the extent to which counter-terrorism law tends to empower the state and disempower the individual, however, a particular democracy- and rights-related anxiety arises here. This is not least because, as a minimum, some of this international fiat

Evaluation of counter-terrorism 121

came from a deeply undemocratic and unrepresentative body – the Security Council – not accustomed (or, it seems, inclined) to taking the rights and democracy implications of its decisions into account. Furthermore, little space for democratic deliberation remained. Even if a state had determined that it had no need for a law criminalizing terrorist financing, or decided that intelligence cooperation with oppressive regimes was incompatible with its democratic values and principles, it was now required to simply implement the law and cooperate in intelligence. Thus, states with little or no history of terrorism found themselves designing, passing and implementing laws, the necessity of which was far from clear, and the field of 'comparative counter-terrorism law' (not to mention a highly lucrative market in security and terrorism consultancy) grew at a startling rate.

This third trend exacerbated many concerns about the undemocratic nature of international and regional organizations (for an overview of these concerns see Chistyakova, 2015). It also of course had implications for domestic democratic principles and processes, as well as for the international conception of the Rule of Law. This is the fourth trend that I want to highlight.

The concept of an international rule of law, it must be conceded, had always been lamentably contested and under-developed, but in the past decade and a half, the 'Rule of Law' has become deeply securitized in international discourses (Lazarus, 2016). From (often largely business-oriented) 'Rule of Law indexes' that are concerned with the security-related stability of a state from the perspective of conducting commerce there, to the inclusion of security and counter-terrorism in Sustainable Development Goal 16a, the 'Rule of Law' no longer looks like a concept encapsulating a liberal legal notion of the restrained state (problematic as that is). Rather, it has 'hardened' into a concept that enables – perhaps even demands – muscular, coercive, intrusive state action to secure the state (materially and metaphorically) and, in the event of state unwillingness or inability, for (international, private or other) proxies to step in and do so. And all this, we are told, in the pursuit of the common good goal of regional and international peace and security.

These four trends provide an important context for understanding not only the expansion of counter-terrorism but also its implications in a post-9/11 world. In this respect, they are a vital framing for the argument about effectiveness that I want to focus on for the rest of this chapter. Through these four trends – and without the need to delve into the detail of any particular law or set of laws – we can see that the expansion of counter-terrorism in the past decade and a half has had, and continues to have, serious implications for human rights (not only of suspected terrorists, but of all of us), for democracy and for the Rule of Law. This is worrying in itself: it points to the high price that is to be paid for 'security'. That price is not the same for all of us, of course, and the uneven societal impacts of counter-terrorism and other forms of security are well documented. These uneven impacts, primarily affecting what Hillyard famously described as 'suspect communities', have themselves developed suspicious communities (Hillyard, 1993). Those suspicious communities should include all of

122 *Fiona de Londras*

us – whether profiled as potential terrorists or 'victims' of radicalization or not – largely because of the problematic nature of the grammar of justification in counter-terrorism. This, then, brings me to effectiveness and its rhetorical antecedent: necessity.

The necessity claim

One thing that is relatively consistent across the different national, regional and international contexts of counter-terrorism is the grammar of justification. Even when unorthodox, previously prohibited or technologically innovative measures and techniques with potentially serious implications for rights, democracy and the Rule of Law are proposed (or are being justified *post hoc*), the key basis for justification tends to be 'necessity'. Strong measures are *necessary* to counter terrorism. Terrorists communicate online, thus data retention, formal Internet regulation and the 'non-contractual cooption' (de Londras, 2013) of ISPs and other online companies are *necessary*. Terrorists use banks for illicit financing, thus asset freezing is *necessary*. Terrorists are trained to withstand 'conventional' interrogation and not reveal information, therefore 'enhanced' interrogation is *necessary*. Terrorists are bent on ideological attack, thus counter-radicalism strategies – even if they severely undermine free speech and coerce confession and denunciation to the detriment of community and social coherence – are *necessary*. Terrorists will radicalize vulnerable persons if they return from ISIS-held territories, therefore exclusion orders and enhanced border surveillance and passenger data sharing are *necessary*.

In this discourse, largely rhetorical but somehow unassailable in its apparent logic, 'necessary' and 'justified' appear to merge into one: that which is necessary is justified, legal or not, democratically approved or not. This rhetorical game is buttressed by tricks of framing (Martin-Mazé and Burgess, 2015): the liberty–security trade-off, the illusion of 'balance', the assertion of exceptionalism (and associated claim of the possibility of normalcy) and the myth of equal sacrifice across the polity all fundamentally rely on the claim of necessity underpinning them. That claim itself, however, relies on – perhaps even insists upon – faith in its veracity. We are encouraged to *trust in* the claim of necessity; to trust that the government would not propose these measures absent that necessity, to trust that the measures *work* to prevent terrorism *and* to maintain the values and structures that underpin the polity. We are asked, in other words, to believe that the measure(s) will *work*. After all, that which does not achieve its function cannot be necessary, and while that which does may not be sufficient in its claim to necessity, that claim is at least *prima facie* established.

In order to truly withstand the threat from terrorism, the polity needs both to emerge/remain/be 'safe' and secured by the state, and to maintain its core constitutionalist values, i.e. not be fundamentally distorted or changed by the measures. In this respect, we implicitly trust the state to quarantine those measures to *bona fide* cases of terrorist threat (which we somehow rarely apprehend being applied to 'us') and to maintain 'normality' throughout the remainder of the state's activities.

Effectiveness

This construction of the contours of the underlying claim itself indicates what a multi-dimensional understanding of effectiveness means in the context of counter-terrorism. In this respect, it points to what I term the meta- and specific objectives of counter-terrorist measures. Meta-objectives include, at the very least, enhancing security, including by not creating backlash or other unintended security vulnerabilities flowing from the measure or measures in question. Furthermore, the maintenance of key constitutionalist principles is a meta-objective of concern. This relates to matters such as the protection of rights, the prevention of 'contagion' of other parts of the apparatus of the state from the 'exceptional' measures of counter-terrorism, and the maintenance and perhaps enhancement of social cohesion, equality dignity and accountability. In order for us properly to assess the effectiveness of a counter-terrorist measure and the robustness of the underlying necessity claim, we must assess all of these matters in as comprehensive, rigorous and open a way as possible, bearing in mind the genuine challenges of counter-terrorism.

So, too, must effectiveness be measured by reference to the specific objectives of the measure in question. It is, thus, appropriate to ask whether counter-terrorist financing laws and other measures actually disrupt terrorist financing, whether restrictions on speech really reduce radicalization, whether citizenship-stripping aids security in any way, and whether those implementing counter-terrorism law and policy have the appropriate protocols, resources, skills and knowledge to achieve the intended ends *without* exceeding the authority conferred by the measure. Critically, we must also ask whether the measures 'work' in a way that less intrusive, less oppressive, less repressive, less 'exceptionalized' measures would not.

A great challenge in counter-terrorism with respect to achieving the meta-objectives outlined above is that we rarely ask these questions in ways that truly address the concerns relating to their oppressiveness. The rhetoric of necessity, in other words, infrequently moves on to a process of justification based on the actuality of effectiveness. In making this observation, let me pause here to note that I make it not from a position of utopian idealism, or one that demands absolute certainty about the effects of measures, or one that disregards the real challenges of security or seriously questions the existence of a terrorist threat at a transnational level. In other words, I do not proceed from a position of unwavering scepticism in which I see all counter-terrorism measures as cynical, self-aggrandizing, bad faith actions by the (supra) state. Instead, my starting point is a more modest one: I expect the (supra) state to act in an informed, reflexive and liberal way vis-à-vis counter-terrorism, just as I expect it to act vis-à-vis everything else. In an era of conspicuous commitment to 'good governance' I question the trend, common across polities, to treat counter-terrorism as an unofficial exception to good governance, answerability and accountability. Rather than simply proliferate counter-terrorism measures seemingly without end, surely the basic tenets of good governance and evidence-based law- and

124   *Fiona de Londras*

policy-making require us to truly assess whether existing measures are effective as our policy and approach – and the nature and scale of the threat – evolve.

The case of technological innovation demonstrates very well why this is important. Technology is generally considered to be a key resource in counter-terrorism, with industry, governments and the EU investing significant resources in research, development, procurement, installation, application and innovation. However, technological approaches to security, including countering terrorism, are not straightforward. These technologies can be, and often are, intrusive, with difficult-to-ascertain end capacities and potentialities, and a high potential for abusive application. Furthermore, they often work within somewhat confounding governance frameworks characterized by Johns as 'list-plus-algorithm', which she writes

> are envisaged doing many useful things: prompting redirection of resources towards areas of greatest need, for instance. Yet, for many, lists-plus-algorithms dissemble as much as they disclose, perturb as much as they excite. Even as they are identified with enhanced capacities of prediction and pre-emption, these practices also evoke a sense of diminished capacity.
>
> (Johns, 2015, p. 128)

State and supra-state institutions are often aware of the sense of unease to which Johns points. In this respect, the European Union, for example, has noted the importance of societal acceptance of technologies applied in the security context. Recognizing a link between core values of the polity and acceptability of technological innovation in security – particularly around civil society participation, rights and the restrained state – the European Commission has determined that a key way to achieve this societal acceptance is to ensure that the impact of new technologies on fundamental rights is thoroughly assessed (European Commission, 2012). This assessment should take place during the technology's research and development – a timing that is intended to allow for rights compliance to be 'designed in' to these technologies. These are, in principle, not unlike the *ex ante* exercises in impact assessment undertaken by the Commission when proposing at least some counter-terrorism measures and approaches. Although the latter arguably focus on providing an evidence-base for political decision-making, they also engage in an exercise of prediction with respect to environmental, economic and – for my purposes, critically – societal impacts, including impacts on fundamental rights (de Londras, 2016). The impact assessments demanded in the field of emerging technologies are also predictive and supposed to consider the future impacts, including societal impacts, of these developing and emerging technologies. Leaving to one side the apparent fallacy of such exercises considering the fact that the final shape, nature, power, reach and context of use of so many technologies cannot possibly be accurately predicted at such an early stage, and considering the fact that the Union appears to have decided on the general effectiveness of technological innovation in the security context (European Commission, 2015, p. 11), these exercises are

Evaluation of counter-terrorism 125

important because they act as a kind of evidence (if such speculative claims can be said to be 'evidence') in advance of the effects of the implementation and use of such technologies.

However, such *ex ante* assessments are challenging in a number of ways, and their challenges are well documented both in general security innovation (de Londras, 2015, 2016) and in technological innovation in the field of security (Bonfanti, 2015). In a factual sense, these exercises are *merely* predictive, i.e. they take into account what 'experts' consider are the likely environmental, economic and societal impacts of proposed measures and technologies. Societal impacts here include impacts on rights, democratic principles, the sense of security and societal values. While economic impacts might be able to be predicted adequately, it is not clear if societal impacts can truly be assessed sufficiently rigorously or quantitatively and, as a result, they tend to be skipped over in what is essentially a pre-legal proportionality analysis contained within the impact assessment. While we might be able to predict that implementing Measure X will cost €4 million per annum spread across 20 stakeholders, for example, we cannot predict that it will lead to an 11% reduction in the effective enjoyment of privacy, or to a 5% reduction in social cohesion. In such circumstances, the qualitative analysis of the impact on rights is not easily assessed alongside the quantitative analysis of the impact on economics, with more 'concrete' data often appearing to receive more analytical weight. This does not mean that those conducting these assessments are not concerned with rights, but rather that such assessments are 'evidence-based' and other forms of impact usually (although not always) carry more weight because they are represented by both more numerous and more verifiable forms of 'evidence' than can usually be presented in respect of the potential impacts on rights.

In other words, and to put it bluntly, *ex ante* impact assessments can only ascertain *predicted* impacts and effectiveness and thus *estimate* the proportionality, effectiveness and appropriateness of the proposed technology or measure. These assessments cannot determine effectiveness or impact as a matter of fact. Their role in the grammar of justification should be to underpin the claim of necessity by making out a *prima facie* case of effectiveness by reference to both meta- and specific objectives, but they do not – and cannot – establish necessity and effectiveness. Rather, that requires an *ex post facto* review of how the measure or technology is actually working, how it is perceived by suspect/suspicious communities, how it is enabling/empowering/overwhelming operational end users, how much it is costing, what its actual impacts on rights (for suspects and others) are and so on. In order to assess effectiveness by reference to both meta- and specific objectives, the *ex post facto* review must be something more than a judicial review. While judicial review is an important constitutionalist process – and plays vital constitutionalist roles in counter-terrorism (de Londras, 2011, 2016) – it cannot assess effectiveness in the broad and vital sense of the term outlined here.

126 *Fiona de Londras*

Ex post facto effectiveness review

In spite of its clear benefits, the *ex post facto* review is rare in the context of counter-terrorism. As I have written elsewhere, '[t]he trend in counter-terrorism is often to implement measures, and then implement more measures, and then more with little or no assessment of the effectiveness and impacts of these policies, laws, instruments and approaches or, sometimes, of their necessity' (de Londras, 2016). Hayes and Jones have illustrated this by reference to a study of the EU's counter-terrorism between 2001 and 2013 (Hayes and Jones, 2014).

They found that of the 88 legally binding measures that were introduced under the rubric of counter-terrorist between 2001 and 2013, 59 contained Commission review clauses and a further nine contained clauses providing for review by the Council. Thus, approximately one third of the legally binding measures introduced in this period of time contained no formal review clause. Of those that did – 62 in total – only 33 of the mandated reviews had taken place on time, a further 10 had not reached their time limit and 16 had not taken place or could not be located (Hayes and Jones, 2014, p. 17). The picture is hardly more positive when one considers the non-legally binding measures. Of eight Agreements, three require review and only one (on the EU-Canada PNR/API Agreement) had taken place (although it cannot be publicly accessed). One of the Common Positions had been reviewed, 11 Decisions had been reviewed, 13 Directives (reflecting the well-established systems for reviewing Directives), nine Framework Decisions and the Joint Action had not been reviewed, and five Regulations had been reviewed. A further five externally contracted reviews had been carried out. Even bearing in mind that formal review of the kind considered by Hayes and Jones is only one form of *ex post facto* review, these statistics are clearly of concern. If we do not assess the effectiveness of these measures, how do we know they work? How do we know they do not exacerbate the security challenges they are designed to address? How do we know if their impact on human rights truly is proportionate not only to their aim but to their effects? How do we know whether the claim of necessity has been borne out?

The answer is simply that we do not know. Certainly, security professionals who use these measures will have an instinct and a professionally informed, experiential awareness of the usefulness and disadvantages of these measures (and that is not always positive (Murphy, Zammit-Borda and Hoyte, 2015)). Furthermore, politicians and policy-makers will have a sense of whether they are 'working' or not. But all of these actors are stakeholders with built-in heuristics, priorities and risk aversion that emanate from their knowledge, position and training and may be difficult to overcome. Furthermore, such 'soft' knowledge is unhelpful from a governance perspective: it is unsubstantiated but cognitively significant and with the capacity to informally influence future policy and law-making processes without a verifiable, comprehensive, fact-based *ex post facto* review to challenge the privileged positioning of practice, information monopolies, expertise and 'insider knowledge'.

Conclusion

In designing mechanisms for reviewing effectiveness, the particular challenges that arise from the constitutional and institutional form of the law- or policy-making entity, which will likely be especially salient in a supra-national context, must be borne in mind. However, the exact nature of the institutional mechanisms for ascertaining the effectiveness of counter-terrorism in any particular polity is a question of design that is ultimately influenced by a commitment to key principles of cooperation (between agencies, states and stakeholders), transparency (which does not have to mean absolutely public transparency but can, rather, be 'tweaked' to accommodate security necessities and *bona fide* concerns) and responsiveness (so that the outcome of the review should be implemented, or at least officially responded to, in some way). To be sure, the challenge of designing and implementing a system that coheres with these principles to ascertain effectiveness is not to be underestimated. However, it seems to me that the *only* way to know whether a measure is effective, taking effectiveness in the rich, multi-dimensional sense that I outline above, is to 'close the public policy loop' by engaging in a comprehensive *ex post facto* review that moves beyond and provides a reality-based counterpoint to the speculative *ex ante* review process. If that is so, and if we wish to move counter-terrorism away from a rhetorical grammar of justification and towards better governance, this challenge is surely one to which we must rise.

References

Bonfanti, M.E., 2015. Let's go for new or emerging security technologies! … What about their impact on individuals and the society? Paper at EISA 9th Pan European Conference on International Relations, on file with author.

Chistyakova, Y., 2015. Democratic legitimacy, effectiveness and the impact of EU counter-terrorism measures. In: F. de Londras and J. Doody, eds., *The impact, legitimacy and effectiveness of EU counter-terrorism*. London: Routledge.

de Londras, F., 2011. *Detention in the 'war on terror': can human rights fight back?* Cambridge: Cambridge University Press.

de Londras, F., 2013. Privatised counter-terrorist surveillance: constitutionalism undermined. In: G. Williams, F.F. Davis and N. McGarrity, eds., *Surveillance, counter-terrorism and comparative* constitutionalism. London: Routledge.

de Londras, F., 2014. Counter-terrorist detention and international human rights law. In: B. Saul, ed., *Research handbook on terrorism and international law*. Cheltenham: Edward Elgar.

de Londras, F., 2015. Governance gaps in EU counter-terrorism: implications for democracy and constitutionalism. In: F. de Londras and J. Doody, eds., *The impact, legitimacy and effectiveness of EU counter*-terrorism. London: Routledge.

de Londras, F., 2016. Accounting for rights in EU counter-terrorism: towards effective review. *Columbia Journal of European Law*, 22(2), pp. 237–274.

de Londras, F., 2017. (Counter-)terrorism and hybridity. In: N. Lemay-Hébert and R. Freedman, eds., *Hybridity: law, culture, and development*. London: Routledge, pp. 58–73.

European Commission, 2012. *Communications security industrial policy action plan for an innovative and competitive security industry* COM (2012) 417.

128 *Fiona de Londras*

European Commission, 2015. *The European agenda on security* COM (2015) 185.

European Court of Human Rights, 2009. *A & Others* v. *United Kingdom* (2009) 49 EHRR 29.

Grozdanova, R., 2014. Terrorism: too elusive a term for an international legal definition? *Netherlands International Law Review*, 61(3), pp. 305–334.

Hayes, B. and Jones, C., 2014. *Report on how the EU assesses the impact, legitimacy and effectiveness of counter-terrorism*. SECILE Consortium.

Hillyard, P., 1993. *Suspect community*. London: Pluto Press.

Johns, F., 2015. Global governance through the pairing of list and algorithm. *Environment and Planning D: Society and Space*, 34(1), pp. 126–149.

Lazarus, L., 2016. *Securing legality*. Oxford: Hart Publishing.

Martin-Mazé, M. and Burgess, J.P., 2015. The societal impact of European counter-terrorism. In: F. de Londras and J. Doody, eds., *The impact, legitimacy and effectiveness of EU counter*-terrorism. London: Routledge, pp. 93–113.

Murphy, C., Zammit-Borda, A. and Hoyte, L., 2015. The perspectives of counter-terrorism operatives on EU counter-terrorism law and policy. In: F. de Londras and J. Doody, eds., *The impact, legitimacy and effectiveness of EU counter-terrorism*. London: Routledge, pp. 157–180.

Strinati, D., 1995. *An introduction to theories of popular culture*. London: Routledge.

UN Security Council, 2001, Resolution 1373.

UN Security Council, 2014, Resolution 2178.

Zedner, L., 2007. Preventive justice or pre-punishment? The case of control orders. *Current Legal Problems*, 60, pp. 174–203.

8 The bleak rituals of progress; or, if somebody offers you a socially responsible innovation in security, just say no

Mark Neocleous

The history of bourgeois modernity is a history in which security occupies centre stage. This is clear from both the long tradition of bourgeois political thought and the extensive reiteration of security by contemporary politicians: from Thomas Hobbes to David Cameron, so to speak. From Hobbes we get the idea that the only solution to the insecurity of the state of nature is a contract exchanging our obedience to the Leviathan for the security it is expected to offer; the state takes centre stage as the provider of the one thing all humans are said to desire. From Hobbes to Cameron: in his 2015 Christmas message to the nation, the British Prime Minister suggested that 'if there is one thing people want at Christmas, it's the security of having their family around them and a home that is safe'. From Hobbes' account of why we flee the state of nature through to Cameron's account of what we all want for Christmas: security, security, security.

Given the predominance of this trope of security, it is easy to think that the Left must have some kind of position here, offering policies or innovations that are somehow meant to be 'socially responsible', which is the general assumption underpinning this book. Such policies or innovations tend to be structured around a number of key principles. The first works with the concept of balance, arguing that security is important but must be balanced with something else such as liberty, or privacy, or democracy. The second approach involves criticizing the 'privatization' of security, with the implication that security should be distinct from the realm of the market and the power of corporations. The third approach starts by pointing to the irrationality that permeates security policy, such as the fact that more people are killed each year by drowning in their own bathtubs than by acts of terrorism, and suggests that once we see through the absurdities of existing security policy, then we will be able to have a more rational security regime. Finally, a fourth approach suggests that current security policies are too discriminatory and that we need to move towards a non-discriminatory security politics which does not target minority groups in an exclusionary fashion.

The problem with these approaches is that they essentially accept the message implicit in the Hobbes-Cameron position about the universal desire for security. They presuppose that what is at stake really is something called 'security' and

130   *Mark Neocleous*

that this is achievable if only security policies were better organized, had more realistic or sensible targets, and were less discriminatory and less subject to the corporate interests working in the security field. In other words, they presuppose that security really is a universal good that could be achieved if the right ('socially responsible') policies were in place. The problem is that once one makes these presumptions, security will always win.

Understanding security's imperative to win requires a grasp of security as the leitmotif of bourgeois modernity. It requires understanding that security can never be disconnected from the powers of war and police to which it belongs, and therefore never disconnected from capital which operates with and through these powers. It requires an understanding of security not as a universal value but as a mechanism of domination deployed by state and capital, and that this deployment of security is part and parcel of the wider politics of fear which underpins bourgeois modernity. Far from being something that could ever be genuinely achieved, security exists for the opportunities it offers to get things done in its name. Security is a mechanism to mobilize, discipline and punish. In other words, security is a power for the fabrication of social order (Neocleous, 2000).

This power lies partly in the fact that in a so-called 'age of rights', security is often presented to us as *the* most fundamental of all rights. According to the United Nations, the fundamental rights of all human beings are 'life, liberty and security'. This claim repeats the revolutionary discourse of rights in the eighteenth century, and one thinker who noticed the implications of such a claim was Marx. In late 1843 in an exchange with Bruno Bauer over 'the Jewish question', Marx runs through the various declarations of the rights of man announced by various states in the late eighteenth century, along with the constitutions which tended to follow such declarations. Marx points out that the rights in question, though revolutionary in some (liberal) ways, are still nonetheless the rights of a member of *bourgeois* society, 'of egoistic man, of man separated from other men and from the community'. 'Let us hear what the most radical Constitution, the Constitution of 1793, has to say', he suggests, and then notes Article 2 of that Constitution: 'These rights, etc., (the natural and imprescriptible rights) are: equality, liberty, security, property'. Marx works through these ideas. Liberty, for example, is 'the power which man has to do everything that does not harm the rights of others', according to one Declaration, or 'being able to do everything which does not harm others', in another. Liberty is thus 'the right to do everything that harms no one else'. J. S. Mill would later confirm this in his articulation of the 'harm principle' in *On Liberty*, but Marx treats it as nothing less than the '*right* of ... separation, the right of the *restricted* individual, withdrawn into himself'. The practical application of this right to liberty is man's right to private property, Marx notes, 'the right to enjoy one's property and to dispose of it at one's discretion ... without regard to other men, independently of society'. This 'right of self-interest ... makes every man see in other men not the *realization* of his own freedom, but the *barrier* to it'. Such observations essentially launch Marx's critique of both rights discourses through the rest of his

The bleak rituals of progress 131

work, but note what he says about security at this moment. On the one hand, the rights discourse is the realization of equality, which is nothing but the equality in which each person is regarded as such a self-sufficient monad. It is also, on the other hand, the *raison d'être* of security. Marx cites Article 8 of the French Constitution of 1793 – 'security consists in the protection afforded by society to each of its members for the preservation of his person, his rights, and his property' – before making the following comment:

> Security is the highest social concept of civil society, the concept of *police*, expressing the fact that the whole of society exists only in order to guarantee to each of its members the preservation of his person, his rights, and his property.

As such, security is the insurance of the egoism of bourgeois society (Marx, 1844/1975, pp. 162–164). Marx has put his finger on the core ideological concept of bourgeois modernity: security. Security underpins and overrides the other egotistic rights associated with bourgeois modernity – liberty, property, equality – in order that bourgeois egoism and capitalist order be guaranteed.

Now, I have previously taken Marx's comment to be a precursor to his claim a few years later in *The Manifesto of the Communist Party* about the bourgeoisie constantly 'revolutionizing the instruments of production, and thereby the relations of production, and with them the whole relations of society'. The 'constant revolutionizing of production, uninterrupted disturbance of all social conditions, everlasting uncertainty and agitation' which accompanies bourgeois rule is what gets described today in the language of insecurity (Marx and Engels, 1848/1984, p. 487). Understood in terms of what has become the most important political trope of contemporary politics, the suggestion seems to be that at some fundamental level the order of capital is an order of *social insecurity*. And yet, at the same time, this permanent insecurity gives rise to a *politics of security*, reinforcing security's place as the fundamental concept of bourgeois society. I have previously argued that this can be interpreted in terms of the ways in which security serves as a key principle of police power in constituting and regulating capital and its modes of coercion and control – the security of the community coincides with the security of the commodity – and have suggested that what is therefore now needed more than anything is nothing less than a critique of security (Neocleous, 2008, also 2000, 2014, 2016; Neocleous and Rigakos, 2011). If we take seriously a comment Marx makes (1843/1975, p. 142) in his debate with Ruge, that the main task before us is not to change the world in the way envisaged by some socialists but, rather, the *ruthless critique of all that exists*, including and especially politics, law and religion, then we might say that for us right now the target of such a ruthless critique has to be that new political religion called 'security'. Such a critique must have as its target all the 'innovations' performed in security's name, including those claiming to be 'socially responsible'.

Security: capital

Capital creates insecurity and insecurity creates a demand and desire for security. To this demand and desire, capital responds with all its usual creativity, in the form of innovation after innovation. Security is therefore highly productive for capital.

To be productive for capital, security must first be translated into the materiality of the commodity. Marx notes that as soon as something emerges as a commodity, it changes into a thing that transcends sensuousness, in such a way that gives the commodity a mystical value. If this is so for the commodity in general, then commodities presented in security terms are at an added advantage as they appear to serve the satisfaction of a very basic, and yet also very indeterminate, human need. But Marx's point is that commodity production per se is far from obvious and trivial. Tracing the contours of the production of security commodities takes us to the heart of the process whereby security becomes fetishistically inscribed in commodified social relations. This is the basis of the security industry.

The expression 'industry' here refers not only to the connection between security and the commodity form but also to the rationalization, distribution, production and consumption of security. It likewise incorporates the spectacle of security.[1] The security industry does not engage in security because of an interest in actually eradicating insecurity. But neither does it do so because it is interested in 'social control' or 'surveillance'. Rather, it has a far more mundane interest: making a profit. To make a profit the security industry must *sell* security. And to sell security it must play on fears and insecurities, must generate further fears and insecurities, and must pander to the idea that our fears and insecurities are very real and must be dealt with in some way. The security industry therefore interpellates consumers as both *sovereign* subjects ('the customer is king') and as *fearful* subjects ('the customer is insecure'). The customer must be reminded time and again of just how insecure they are, revealing more than anything the extent to which capital has found a way of dominating and terrorizing human beings within their very hearts and souls. This is one reason why struggles against 'security measures' alone are always so limiting: without connecting security to capital, such struggles never address the basic antagonism of bourgeois society.

The security industry is thus where capital and security come to contemplate themselves in a world of their own making, playing a key role in the fabrication of the much wider culture of fear and insecurity that is used to shore up both state and capital. Where the state uses fear and insecurity to sustain support for the national security project, the security industry turns the fear and insecurity into the consumption of commodities. Where the security state thus perpetually offers more and more 'solutions' in the form of new security policies, the security industry offers 'solutions' in entirely commodified forms, as more and more commodities are simply marketed as solutions to one insecurity after another. The security industry thus uses its purported concern for human beings and their security to reinforce the logic of both security and the commodity form across the face of society.

The bleak rituals of progress 133

To the extent that both capital and the state live off the production of fear and insecurity, they must also ensure that security is something never really achieved. Behind the slogan 'Security now!' lies the real double-sided message: on the one hand, 'Security with the next security product' (the message from capital); on the other hand, 'Security with the next security measure' (the message from the state). Yet both the security industry and the security state perpetually cheat us of what has been promised. The promissory note is endlessly prolonged, revealing that, ultimately, the promise is illusory: all that is confirmed is that the real target will never be reached. Security is revealed to be an illusion.

Part of security's illusory power requires a passive acceptance of all the things done in security's name and all the things state and capital want us to take most seriously as needing securing: property and commodity, law and order. Security wants us to believe that nothing other than that which is called security is good, or at least that whatever else might be considered good is nowhere nearly as good as security itself. Moreover, it wants us to believe that that which is good must be secure. Security thereby subjugates living humans to security itself. In so doing, it masks the real impoverishment of human life. Worse, it functions in such a way that this impoverishment is understood as the very thing that needs to be secured. If the main task of ideology is to get us to believe that 'the bourgeois way of thinking is the normal way of thinking' (Marx, 1859/1987, p. 315), then security is ideology par excellence, integral to the system of domination which now encloses the world, where each individual trembles lest they be found guilty of transgressing the boundaries imposed by security and its demands. This is why security is so demanding: it is nearly impossible to unravel the demands that security imposes on us and the immense labour that security incessantly performs on us, a labour that in turn produces new demands on us as subjects, new norms by which we are measured, new targets towards which we should be striving, new mechanisms through which hopes and dreams are to be thwarted.

Witness, for example, the phenomenon that has been described as neoliberalism. Much can and has been made of the ways in which neoliberalism involves a transformation of the individual: 'economics are the method; the object is to change the heart and soul', as Margaret Thatcher (*Sunday Times*, 1981) once put it. Taking such a claim seriously means reading neoliberalism not simply in terms of its *destructive power*, for example in destroying certain kinds of rights and institutions, but also in terms of its *productive power*: in its ability to *create* new kinds of social relations, new ways of living and new political subjects. The literature on the new neoliberal subject recognizes more than anything that what is being produced is an entrepreneurial self and a productive subject: a monetized, atomized and calculating subject that is required and expected to endlessly perform as a neoliberal subject in the social realm as well as in the marketplace (Dardot and Laval, 2013). This production of new subjectivities, however, is also very much an *orientation of the subject around security*: new political subjects forged through security, operating for security and organized around security. In other words, security-conscious neoliberal subjects. The connection between security and

134   *Mark Neocleous*

capital is thus integral to the neoliberal revolution and part of neoliberalism's productive power and disciplinary core. (As with so many aspects of neoliberalism, what is of most interest is its disciplinary moment, and at the heart of this disciplinary moment lies the logic of security.) The explosion and expansion of security in the last two decades, while conventionally connected to the problem of terrorism (the 'war on terror'), might just as properly be connected to the attempt to engrain neoliberalism into the hearts and minds of political subjects.

Moreover, because the neoliberal subject is expected to be an *active* subject, this activity is also expected to respond to the demands of security as well as the demands of capital. As is well known, under neoliberalism it is no longer enough for us to simply work, earn our money, go home and spend it. Now we must believe in the work we are doing and actively show that we believe in it, identifying with the organization and signing up to the company's mission, vision and values. The neoliberal workplace has become a 'community of desire', as Frédéric Lordon puts it, and yet this poses a problem for capital, which constantly questions the worker's desire. In Lordon's example: the employee-subject swears that they have no other passion than the manufacture of yoghurt, our company's business, but *can we really believe them*? (Lordon, 2015, p. 84). The answer has to be no, and so the expected desire must be constantly expressed, measured and assessed, since it is always in danger of fading. A similar point might be made about the neoliberal polity, and likewise about the neoliberal security state: the citizen-subject swears that they have no other interest than the security of the social order, but *can we really believe them*? The answer must again be no,[2] and so the expected desire must also be constantly expressed, measured and assessed, since it is always in danger of fading. Herein lies the basis for all the actions we are now being trained to undertake as security-conscious neoliberal subjects, such as being trained in 'resilience', being taught to be constantly 'prepared for emergency', and being encouraged to report any friends, family, lovers, neighbours and colleagues who we suspect might be doing something 'suspicious' (Neocleous, 2013, 2016, 2017). Part of the novelty of neoliberalism lies precisely in the idea that this active subject is not expected to remain content with the simple exchange of security for obedience, but, rather, is to be actively mobilized around the logic of security. Security has become a neoliberal mobilization regime: the people mobilized in the name of security as well as capital.

Such mobilization is yet another way of incorporating the people into security and another way in which security expresses its desire to exist without reply, just like capital and the state. Part of the illusion of security is that we are expected to bow down before it without even asking what it is or how it came to be granted such a status. To exist without reply, security seeks to nullify all dissent and suppress any rebellion *even before such dissent and rebellion have begun.* Any objections or resistance to any of the policies – not least the economic policies – being carried out by the powers which claim to exercise security on our behalf are met either with security measures of the most coercive kind or with the expectation that reason must abase itself before it – all our critical faculties set aside as security and its leading defenders tell us to shut up, listen and obey. Those

The bleak rituals of progress 135

arguing against austerity, for example, are treated first and foremost as a threat to national security. Thus, far from security being emancipation, as some people working in the academic sector of the security industry like to claim *and which is the very belief that security wants us to hold*, the articulation of security as an overarching principle of politics – the idea, in other words, that security is the absolute foundation of all politics, or that security has to be the starting point for any political thought, or that security is the grounds on which we must accept the protection of the state, or that what all of us would most like for Christmas is security – is nothing less than the articulation of a demand for obedience. Security is in this sense central to the containment of social change, nothing less than the principle and process of pacification, if by 'pacification' we understand not simply the military crushing of resistance but, rather, the *fabrication of social order* (Neocleous, 2011, 2017; Neocleous, Rigakos and Wall, 2013).

What does this obedience in the name of security produce? The answer is not difficult: obedience itself. Obedience produces obedience, as Foucault once commented (2014, p. 270) about what he called 'pastoral power'. It reproduces itself as a system of obedience. That is, one accepts the principle of security in order to become obedient and one reproduces this state of obedience in a striving for the mythical state of security. Hence one is expected to manage oneself in the way that a security operative would have us be managed. This is the very point to which Hobbes alludes in the final paragraph of *Leviathan*; it is the very same point understood by all contemporary politicians when they speak the language of security; and it is the point implicit in much of the discourse and policies surrounding terrorism, which is why so much anti-terror legislation concerns itself with the obedience of the population. Obedience thereby becomes a permanent way of being, and we are encouraged and expected to believe that obedience is essential to the security of the subject. Obedience becomes fundamental to the principle of *raison d'état*, demanded by the state for security reasons, and our training in obedience a training of and for political order. And, given the security–commodity nexus, what we are being made obedient for is nothing other than the domination of our lives by capital.

Security, then, demands that we bow down to security. It demands that we feel secure in our insecurity as bourgeois subjects but also insecure in our security as bourgeois subjects. It demands that we commit ourselves not to making history but, rather, to the eternal recurrence of the same: to securing capital and the state rather than anything against it or opposed to them. Like capital, security wants us to believe that it is our fate.

Opening his book *Politics and Fate*, Andrew Gamble asks: 'If politics were at an end, if this was our fate, what would this mean for us?' (2000, p. 1). One answer: it would mean nothing less than being stuck in an endless security experience. 'How was your security experience today?', the questionnaire at Heathrow airport demands, after making us undergo a series of security rituals. An endless security experience, then, but one in which we are constantly asked to assess, measure and confirm our happiness in being able to participate in the rituals and thus in the process to confirm the extent to which security dominates

136 *Mark Neocleous*

our lives. A second answer to Gamble's question: it would mean being subjected to one security innovation after another, including those innovations sold to us as being somehow 'socially responsible'.

Security: innovation

Innovation is one of the dominant ideas of our time. 'Innovation is everywhere', notes Benoît Godin.

> In the world of goods (technology) certainly, but also in the realm of words: innovation is discussed in the scientific and technical literature, in social sciences like history, sociology, management and economics, and in the humanities and arts. Innovation is also a central idea in the popular imaginary, in the media, in public policy, and is part of everybody's vocabulary .
> (Godin, 2008, p. 5)

As Godin notes, innovation has become the emblem of modern society and a panacea for resolving any and all of society's problems.

Despite its close association with the seemingly neutral terrain of technology, innovation is in fact a deeply political concept. But as a political concept, its connotations have changed dramatically over the centuries. 'Innovation' was for centuries a pejorative term, because innovation itself was regarded as a vice. Innovation, Godin notes, was regulated by Kings for centuries, forbidden by law and punished. Advice books and treatises for Princes and courtiers support this understanding, and include instructions not to innovate. Books of manners and sermons urge people not to meddle with innovation, and bishops visit parishes to make sure that the instruction is followed. From the Renaissance onward, innovation is also a linguistic weapon used by political writers and pamphleteers against their enemies (Godin, 2013, p. 8, 2015, pp. 5, 10–11).

Entrenched ideas about the power of 'tradition' and 'order' meant that the innovator and innovation were suspect. On the one hand, in religious terms, innovation was considered heretical: 'innovation and heresy were practically synonymous' (Preus, 1972, p. 2). On the other hand, in political terms, innovation was considered revolutionary, as witnessed by Edmund Burke's *Reflections on the Revolution in France*, in which Burke castigates the 'spirit of innovation' found among revolutionaries. According to Burke, innovation is the result of a 'selfish temper', 'confined views' and a 'furious spirit'; a good and proper politics consists in a 'sullen resistance to innovation' (Burke, 1790/1968, pp. 119, 181, 211, 237, 320, 325, 1795/1992, p. 271). The fact that no revolutionary ever thought of describing their own politics in terms of 'innovation' tells us that 'innovation' was a term used pejoratively by anti-revolutionaries against those questioning the political order. Innovation was thus a word used for polemical purposes and in a pejorative way, 'a linguistic weapon used against an enemy: the revolutionary, the republican and, in the nineteenth century, the socialist' (Godin, 2013, p. 17, also pp. 6–8, 11–12, 2015, p. 5).

The bleak rituals of progress   137

All of that gradually changed with the conceptual revolution associated with the emergence of new time (*neue Zeit*) or modernity (*Neuzeit*) in the late eighteenth century. Core to the formation of the new time of modernity is what Reinhart Koselleck identifies as a shift in which key concepts play on the general criterion of modernity's 'dynamization' and 'acceleration'. Such concepts no longer simply define a given state of affairs but instead 'reach into the future' (Koselleck, 2004, p. 80, 2002, pp. 154–169). The concept which most clearly captures Koselleck's point about dynamism and the future is the one on which he focuses, namely 'revolution', but the point applies equally to 'innovation' (Nowotny, 2008). In the history of the concept 'innovation', a transition period therefore occurs between the late eighteenth century and the mid-nineteenth century in which an increasingly neutral use of the term coexists with the pejorative use, and then the pejorative use slowly dies out as an increasingly positive understanding of the term coincides with the neutral, to the point that by the twentieth century, innovation had become a more or less entirely positive term (Godin, 2015, p. 16). The shift coincides with the embrace of innovation by both capital and the state. People start to talk about the age of industrial capital as a new 'age of innovation'. The 'spirit of innovation' no longer describes revolutionaries seeking to overthrow the existing order but rather those who seek to contribute to its continual 'improvement' and 'civilization' (two other keywords in capitalist mentality – see Neocleous, 2014). The 'spirit of innovation' becomes part and parcel of the 'spirit of capitalism', as innovation itself becomes the foundation for something called 'progress', a category which is itself 'specifically calibrated to cope with modern experiences, namely that traditional experiences are surpassed by new ones with astonishing speed' (Koselleck, 2002, pp. 219–220). Capital is a category of movement and 'innovation' a term that gives voice to this movement, in the process becoming part and parcel of bourgeois ideology.

Now, on the one hand, this indicates that innovation has become part of the self-understanding of the bourgeois revolution, for as well as implying technological advance, it also connotes all those things which the bourgeoisie likes to see in itself as a class: creativity, productivity, liberty and progress. This is summed up most precisely in Joseph Schumpeter's *The Theory of Economic Development* (1911), which identifies innovation as *the* central feature of economic development and the entrepreneur as *the* central figure behind it (Schumpeter, 1911/1983). Bourgeois thought has transformed this into a more generalized theory of commerce (albeit rooted in a certain conception of technology) and then generalized it further still into ideas about 'organizational innovation', in which the 'spirit of innovation' is assumed to reside not so much in individuals but in the organization itself. (Such spirit was initially associated with the capitalist firm, but very quickly became applied to the organization per se.) From there the term has come to incorporate positive changes in politics, law and culture as well, reflecting its fundamental place in society's conception of itself. Either way, 'innovative' is now a form of praise and people are criticized for not being innovative enough. Individuals, organizations, companies, capital, nations and states are all expected to know what innovation means, to treat it as an unconditional good and to take part

138 *Mark Neocleous*

in the process (Nowotny, 2008, p. 141; Godin, 2013, p. 18). Rather like security, innovation has become more or less a duty. On the one hand, then, 'innovation' has become a concept around which capital and the state operate and cooperate.

On the other hand, socialists have sought to give innovation a 'social' twist. Starting in the nineteenth century, social reforms began to be conceived of as social innovations and, at the same time, social innovations began to be considered in terms of their contribution to social reform – or, better still, considered in terms of their contribution to something understood by social reformers as 'progress'. I suspect that the commitment to socially responsible innovations (in security or anything else) has something to do with the idea of progress. Koselleck's claim that 'since the nineteenth century, it has become difficult to gain political legitimacy without being progressive at the same time' (Koselleck, 2002, p. 230) applies in particular to the ways in which social reformers ('progressives') like to use key concepts such as innovation. Thus, alongside the discourse of technological or commercial innovation, 'one now hears discourses on "social innovation", meaning either major advances in the social sciences, policy/institutional reforms for the betterment of society, or solutions to social needs and problems, coming from the community sectors among others' (Godin, 2008, p. 46). For progressives, the concept of progress contains the idea that innovations can and should be a good thing, so long as they are delivered in the spirit of liberty and democracy. For progressives this means that innovation has to be, in the style of most of the contributions to this book, *socially responsible*. To put it in Arendtian terms for a moment (Arendt, 1963), one might say that socially responsible innovations are a means of importing 'the social question' into the concept of innovation.

How does this affect the claims made here about security? If 'innovation is a concept that everyone understands spontaneously – or *thinks* he understands' (Godin, 2015, p. 3, emphasis added), then that is even more the case with what we are expected to accept as a 'socially responsible innovation', and it is especially the case with socially responsible innovation in something else that we *think* we understand, namely security. Now, one might note here Helga Nowotny's point that the concept of security and the idea of a rationality promising security are inherently unable to keep pace with the acceleration and expansion of possibilities opened up by the world of continuous innovation (Nowotny, 2008, pp. 15, 39–40, 140). In other words, continual innovation surely contributes to the constant change and everlasting uncertainty that is the foundation of much that goes by the name of 'insecurity'. But that is not my point. My point, rather, is that if *socially responsible innovation* is a concept specifically calibrated to cope with the quintessentially modern experience of the constant revolutionizing of the instruments and relations of production – the fact that 'all that is solid melts into air', in Marx and Engels's felicitous phrase – in such a way that something 'progressive' might still come out of the experience, so we might say that the idea of socially responsible innovation *in security* is an idea specifically calibrated to cope with the quintessentially modern experience of the constant revolutionizing of everything that goes under the name of security.

The bleak rituals of progress 139

Yet to organize and mobilize in the name of socially responsible innovation in security is nonetheless to *organize and mobilize in the name of security*. Moreover, as I have been trying to suggest in the first half of this chapter, it is likewise to *mobilize in the name of capital*. What 'socially responsible innovation in security' gives us, then, is little more than yet another way of participating in the logic of security. Adopting a term straight out of the discourse of capital ('innovation'), and adding to it one of the key terms of corporate neoliberal power (namely 'corporate social responsibility'), socially responsible innovations in security appear to be little more than new ways of rendering the social over to the powers of state and capital.

One might extend this observation by pointing out that although it is generally assumed that the whole point of innovation is that it surprises – 'the greater the surprise, the more innovative the idea' (Nowotny, 2008, p. 103) – rarely is anything actually genuinely surprising offered in socially responsible innovations in security. Quite the opposite, in fact: accepting entirely the logic of security, all such innovations do is try and moderate this logic by somehow recognizing 'privacy' or 'liberty', or by not being too discriminatory or exclusionary, or by being less under the corporate powers within the security industry. Ultimately, the least surprising thing of all happens: *security still wins*. Worse, security wins by having the whole of the social offered up to it, and offered up to it by the new 'socially progressive' advisors to Princes, those whose political vision commits us to what we are told must be our fate: one security experience after another, one security scare after another, one recovery from each security scare after another, one security innovation after another.

The more dominant a concept becomes, the more unimaginable the means by which those living under its spell might break that domination. In the case of security, the only way to imagine breaking its domination is to begin with its ruthless critique. To advocate socially responsible innovation in security is to advocate conformity rather than critique. If somebody offers you a socially responsible innovation in security, just say no.

Notes

1 The spectacle of terrorism is one part of the spectacle of security, just as the terrorism industry is in fact one part of the much larger and older security industry (see Neocleous, 2016).
2 The answer has to be 'no' because to unreservedly believe anyone is committed to the security of the social order would be to rest assured that this person is not and never could be a security threat. But no-one can ever genuinely occupy that position. This is why even the politicians who run the system are placed under surveillance.

References

Arendt, H., 1963. *On revolution*. New York: Viking.
Burke, E., 1790/1968. *Reflections on the revolution in France*. Harmondsworth: Penguin.
Burke, E., 1795/1992. Letter to William Elliot, 26 May, 1795. In: E. Burke, *Further reflections on the revolution in France*. Indianapolis, IN: Liberty Fund.

140 *Mark Neocleous*

Dardot, P. and Laval, C., 2013. *The new way of the world: on neoliberal society*. London: Verso.

Foucault, M., 2014. *On the government of the living: lectures at the Collège de France, 1979–1980*. Houndmills, Basingstoke: Palgrave.

Gamble, A., 2000. *Politics and fate*. Cambridge: Polity.

Godin, B., 2008. *Innovation: the history of a category*. Working Paper No. 1. Montreal, Quebec: Project on the Intellectual History of Innovation.

Godin, B., 2013. *Innovation after the French Revolution, or, innovation transformed: from word to concept*. Working Paper No. 14. Montreal, Quebec: Project on the Intellectual History of Innovation.

Godin, B., 2015. *Innovation: a conceptual history of an anonymous concept*. Working Paper No. 21. Montreal, Quebec: Project on the Intellectual History of Innovation.

Koselleck, R., 2002. *The practice of conceptual history: timing history, spacing concepts*. Stanford, CA: Stanford University Press.

Koselleck, R., 2004. *Futures past: on the semantics of historical time*. New York: Columbia University Press.

Lordon, F., 2015. *Willing slaves of capital: Spinoza and Marx on desire*. London: Verso.

Marx, K., 1843/1975. Letters from *Deutsch-Französische Jahrbücher*. In: K. Marx and F. Engels, *Collected works, vol. 3*. London: Lawrence and Wishart.

Marx, K., 1844/1975. On the Jewish question. In: K. Marx and F. Engels, *Collected works, vol. 3*. London: Lawrence and Wishart.

Marx, K., 1859/1987. *A contribution to the critique of political economy*. In: K. Marx and F. Engels, *Collected works, vol. 29*. London: Lawrence and Wishart.

Marx, K. and Engels, F., 1848/1984. *The manifesto of the communist party*. In: K. Marx and F. Engels, *Collected works, vol. 6*. London: Lawrence and Wishart.

Neocleous, M., 2000. *The fabrication of social order: a critical theory of police power*. London: Pluto Press.

Neocleous, M., 2008. *Critique of security*. Edinburgh: Edinburgh University Press.

Neocleous, M., 2011. Security as pacification. In: M. Neocleous and G. Rigakos, eds., *Anti-security*. Ottawa: Red Quill Books, pp. 23–56.

Neocleous, M., 2013. Resisting resilience. *Radical Philosophy*, 178, pp. 2–7.

Neocleous, M., 2014. *War power, police power*. Edinburgh: Edinburgh University Press.

Neocleous, M., 2016. *The universal adversary: security, capital and 'The enemies of all mankind'*. Abingdon, Oxon: Routledge.

Neocleous, M., 2017. Fundamentals of pacification theory: twenty-six articles. In: T. Wall, P. Saberi and W. Jackson, eds., *Destroy, build, secure: readings on pacification*. Ottawa: Red Quill Books.

Neocleous, M. and Rigakos, G. eds., 2011. *Anti-security*. Ottawa: Red Quill Press.

Neocleous, M., Rigakos, G. and Wall, T., 2013. On pacification: introduction to the special issue. *Socialist Studies/Études socialistes*, 9(2), pp. 1–6.

Nowotny, H., 2008. *Insatiable curiosity: innovation in a fragile future*. Cambridge, MA: MIT Press.

Preus, J., 1972. Theological legitimation for innovation in the Middle Ages. *Viator*, 3, pp. 1–26.

Schumpeter, J., 1911/1983. *The theory of economic development: an inquiry into profits, capital, credit, interest, and the business cycle*. New Brunswick, NJ: Transaction Publishers.

Sunday Times, 1981. Mrs Thatcher: the first two years. *The Sunday Times*, 3 May.

Index

Page numbers in **bold** denote tables, those in *italics* denote figures.

Abrams, P. 97
Agre, P.E. 28

Barber, B. 86
Bauer, Bruno 130
Bauwens, Tom 85–96
behavioural profiling 78
Berlin, Isaiah 28
biometrics 49–50
Blok, V. 6, 18
Bozzoli, C. 64
Brandeis, L.D. 28
Burgess, J. Peter 1–11, 12–21
burglary *see* theft prevention
Burke, Edmund 136

Cameron, David 129
CCTV 78, 106, 109
Clarke, Roger 28
Collingridge dilemma 6
Cook, I.R. 108
counter-terrorism 10, 117–128; changes to
    international law developed by United
    Kingdom and United States 118–119;
    domestic counter-terrorism law and
    international influences 120–121;
    effectiveness of 123–125; *ex post facto*
    effectiveness review 126, 127; impact
    assessments 124–125; justification for
    counter-terrorist measures 122, 123;
    laws and policies, increase of 117; rule
    of law concept 121; and technological
    innovation 124–125; transnationalism in
    terrorism 118; UN Security Council
    Resolution 1373 119–120
crime 65, 68; fear of 66, 69, 74, 75, 76, 79;
    see also theft prevention

data exchange systems 63
Davis, Fred 51
De Saille, S. 2
detection 31–32, *31*
DNA-database 78
drones: context of use 34; interpretative
    flexibility 34; killer drones 33;
    privacy and security in drones,
    understanding of 36–37, 38; relevant
    social groups 34, 37–38; socio-technical
    construction of 33–38; study
    conclusions 37–38; study research
    method 35–36; unmanned aerial systems
    (UASs) 34–35

East Jerusalem, national parks *see* security
    providers, state effects of, Jerusalem
encryption technologies 26
European Charter of Fundamental Rights
    7, 39n2
European Commission 5–6, 12, 17–18,
    124; Security Industrial Strategy 21
European Convention of Human Rights 9

Finn, R.L. 28
Foucault, M. 135
French Constitution 1793 130, 131
Friedewald, Michael 25–43

Gadamer, Hans-Georg 88
Gamble, Andrew 135–136
Godin, Benoît 12–13, 136
Greenberg, R. 101
Guston, D.H. 4
Gwiazda, M. 101

Hann, C. 97, 105, 112

142 *Index*

Hansen, T.B. 98
Hardyns, Wim 1–11, 44–62
Hayes, B. 126
Hillyard, P. 121
Hobbes, Thomas 129, 135
home automation systems 48–49
Hoorde, Kim Van 44–62
Hoven, Jeroen van den 18
Huddy, L. 67
human rights 9, 10; and counter-terrorism 118–119, 121

identification 31–32, *31*
innovation: commercial innovation 2–3; distinction from invention 16–17; European responsible innovation 16–18; insecurity as a driver of innovation 19–20; notion of 12–13; as part of a bourgeois revolution 137–138; as a political concept 136–137; responsible innovation 2–3, 4–5, 6–7, 13–14; security challenges and responsible innovation 18–20; security innovation, ethics of 1–2; and social reform 138; and value 3–4
Innovation Contested: The Idea of Innovation over the Centuries (Godin) 12–13
internet: influence on crime 44; Internet of Things (IoT) 44, 47–48, 51–52, 52–53, 54–55, 58–59; intrusion of, upon our 'things' 47–48; scenarios of the Internet of Things in private homes 48–50
Israeli Nature and Parks Authority 100, 101–102

Johns, F. 124
Jones, C. 126

Koselleck, Reinhart 137, 138
Krti, L. 97, 105, 112

Land, K.C. 69
Lemmens, P. 6, 18
Lerner, J.S. 64
liberalism 19; neoliberalism 133–134
Lieshout, Marc van 25–43
Londreas, Fiona de 117–128
Lordon, Frédéric 134

Macnaghten, P. 4, 6
The Manifesto of the Communist Party (Marx) 131
Marx, Karl 130–131, 132, 133

mayors and security 86; interpretative repertoire of policy 89, **90**; local governance of security in Belgium 86–87; prohibition to party as an innovative security practice 91–92; repertoire of justice 89, **90**; repertoire of responsiveness 89, **90**; securitization by regulation 92–93; understanding the experience of having to provide security 87–90, **90**, 94; zonal bans 92–93
Mbembe, J. 108
Medvecky, F. 2
Meintjes, L. 108
migration 14–15
Mill, J.S. 130
Mitchell, T. 98, 104–105
modernity 13, 17, 129–130, 131, 133, 137
moral philosophy 5
Müller, C. 64

Neocleous, Mark 129–140
neoliberalism 133–134
The New Democracy (Schinkel) 92
Nowotony, Helga 138

obedience 135
Ong, A. 98
Owen, R. 4, 6

Pauw, Evelien De 44–62
Pelle, S. 2, 5
Politics and Fate (Gamble) 135–136
Ponnet, Koen 1–11
PRISMS project 25–26, 27–28, 28, 36, 37
privacy 1, 8, 29; anxiety and changes of opinion on use of SOSTs 75; anxiety and use of SOSTs 67; attitude changes, SOSTs study 71–72, **71**, **72**, 75–77; attitudes and acceptance of new technologies 64; breaches of 56–57; definitions of 28; dimensions of 28–29; drivers of and barriers to privacy and security technologies 29, 32–33, **32**, 38; and drones 36–37, 38–39; in EU research programmes 29–32, *30*, *31*; identifying the occurrence of privacy and security in research activities 29; inscription of social norms in technology 26; keywords 29, 31–32, *31*; Paris attacks and changes in attitudes to SOSTS 64–66; post-hoc analyses, SOSTs study 73–75, **73**, **74**; privacy-control trade-off 65, 66, 68, 71, **71**, 72, **72**, 73–74, **73**, **74**, 75–76, 77, 78–79;

relationship between privacy and security 25–26; research and the relationship between privacy and security 27–29; research questions for the study on SOSTs 66–67; results of the SOSTs study 70–75; social construction of privacy and security technologies 25–43; SOSTs study, sample profile 70–71, **71**; students' opinions on trust, risk-perception and SOSTs 66, 74–75; study on SOSTs, design and sample characteristics 67–70; and surveillance oriented security technologies (SOSTs) 63–64; Surveillance Privacy and Security project (SURPRISE) 63, 76; vignettes regarding SOSTs used in the study 77–80

Pullan, W. 101

radio frequency identification 77–78
Reber, B. 2, 5
Reflections on the Revolution in France (Burke) 136
Reniers, Genserik 1–11
responsibility: responsible innovation 2–3, 4–5, 6–7, 13–14, 16–18; responsible research and innovation concept (RRI) 17–18; security challenges and responsible innovation 18–20
risk 2, 66, 69, 74–75, 76, 79
Rotenberg, M. 28
Rountree, P.W. 69
rule of law 10, 117, 121

Schinkel, Willem 92
Schumpeter, Joseph P. 16, 17, 18, 137
security: and bourgeois modernity 129–130, 131, 133; and capital 131, 132–136, 137; dimensions of 27–28; drivers of and barriers to privacy and security technologies 29, 32–33, **32**, 38; and drones 36–37, 38–39; in EU research programmes 29–32, *30*, *31*; European security landscape and threats 14–16; as a fundamental right 130–131; identifying the occurrence of privacy and security in research activities 29; as an illusion 133; imagining future security 12–21; and innovation 136–139; (in)security, definition of 87–89; insecurity as a driver of innovation 19–20; keywords 29; local governance of security in Belgium

86–87; and neoliberalism 133–134; novelty, role of 16; and obedience 135; principles of and approaches to 129–130; prohibition to party as an innovative security practice 91–92; public and private security provision 97–114; relationship between privacy and security 25–26; research and development 16; research and the relationship between privacy and security 27–29; and responsible innovation 13–14; responsible innovation in Europe 16–18; securitization 5, 9, 85–96; security challenges and responsible innovation 18–20; security industry 132–133; understanding the experience of having to provide security 87–90, **90**, 94; zonal bans 92–93

security providers, state effects of, Jerusalem 9–10, 97–114; City of David site 101–107, *102*, 110–111, *113*; conceptual approach to the state 97–99; Dung Gate, Old City 108–110, *109*; effects on daily life for Palestinians 102–105, 108–111; firearms use of 105; Jerusalem as a divided city 99–100; legal appeal against private security guards 107; methodology of the study 99; national parks 100; outsourcing of security provision 99, 107, 112; private security and the Valley of Sweet Water 101–108, *106*; security encounters and deliberate friction 108–111

Sharon, Arieh 101–102
Smit, Wim 1–11
sovereignty 9–10, 98–99, 107–108, 112, 113
Stahl, B.C. 5
Stilgoe, J. 4, 6
Stone, D. 85
surveillance 5, 31–32, *31*
surveillance oriented security technologies (SOSTs) 8–9, 51, 63–82; anxiety and use of SOSTs 67, 75; attitude changes, SOSTs study 64–66, 71–72, **71**, **72**, 75–77; attitudes and acceptance of new technologies 64; post-hoc analyses, SOSTs study 73–75, **73**, **74**; research questions for the study on SOSTs 66–67; results of the SOSTs study 70–75; SOSTs study, sample profile 70–71, **71**; students' opinions on trust, risk-perception and SOSTs 66, 74–75;

144   *Index*

surveillance oriented security technologies (SOSTs) *continued*
study on SOSTs, design and sample characteristics 67–70; vignettes regarding SOSTs used in the study 77–80
Surveillance Privacy and Security project (SURPRISE) 51, 63, 76

Taebi, B. 4
technological change: social construction of technology (SCOT) 34; speed of 6; technology acceptance model (TAM) 51; technology optimism 80
terrorism 7, 12, 25–26, 63–82; anxiety and use of SOSTs 67, 75; attitude changes, SOSTs study 64–66, 71–72, **71, 72,** 75–77; design and sample characteristics, SOSTs study 67–70; fear of 79–80; Paris attacks 64–66; post-hoc analyses, SOSTs study 73–75, **73, 74**; research questions for the study on SOSTs 66–67; results of the SOSTs study 70–75; SOSTs study, sample profile 70–71, **71**; students' opinions on trust, risk-perception and SOSTs 66, 74–75; Surveillance Privacy and Security project (SURPRISE) 51, 63, 76; vignettes regarding SOSTs used in the study 77–80; *see also* counter-terrorism
theft prevention 8, 44–62; application restrictions of a new technology for burglary prevention 57–58; biometrics 49–50; burglary and theft, perceptions of 52–53; burglary prevention and electronic security 53–55; citizen perspectives and knowledge of experts 52–58; citizens' lack of knowledge of new technologies 58–59; crime-enhancing or crime-fighting technology and domestic burglary 47–52; electronic and technological systems 53; environmental design and partners network 59–60; home automation systems 48–49; internet, influence on crime 44; internet's intrusion on our

'things' 47–48; privacy breaches, concerns for 56–57; recommendations for future theft prevention 59–60; research objectives and methodology 45–47; scenarios of the Internet of Things in private homes 48–50; security and prevention, perspectives on responsibility for 55–56; social perception and acceptance of technology 50–52; supply of information 60; technological innovation, influence on crime 44–45; track and trace 50; unsecured wireless networks, problems of 60
Theory of Economic Development (Schumpeter) 16, 137
track and trace 50
Trouillot, M. 97, 105, 112
trust 7, 51, 52; in necessity of security 122; in public authorities 64, 65, 66, 68–69, **71, 72, 72, 73, 74,** 76, 77, 78; in technology 19

UN Security Council 121; Resolution 1373 119–120
unified theory of acceptance and use of technology (UTAUT) 51
unmanned aerial systems (UASs) *see* drones
unmanned aerial vehicles (UAVs) *see* drones

Valdivia, W.D. 4
values 20–21; personal values 5; public values 4
Valverde, Marianne 88
Vandenbogaerde, Ellen 63–82
Venkatesh, V. 51
Vermeersch, Hans 44–62, 63–82
Volinz, Lior 97–114
von Schomberg, R. 6

Warren, S.D. 28
Westin, Alan 28
Whowell, M. 108
Wright, D. 28